1. Introduction to India

Are you planning a tour to Ind
incredibly different messages
visitors to the country find it amazing while others find that it
was one bad experience. Some love the colors, the noise,
the people, the food and the spirituality it has to offer while
others find it smelly, polluted and believe that everyone in
India is there to cheat them in some way or the other.

No matter what you read or hear, that fact is that nothing can
prepare you for India no matter how many trips you have
made to the country. Even for the locals; India is a vast and
diverse concept - comprising of people speaking a multitude
of languages, following a variety of religious beliefs, customs,
dress codes, food habits and festivals and much more. You
must plan your trip carefully to make the most of it as a
traveler.

Here's a preliminary introduction to the country

Ethnic communities of India

The ethnic communities of India includes Negroids (the first to arrive in India), Pro-Australoids (they laid the foundation of Indian civilization), Mongoloids (those who live in the North East of India close to the Chinese border), Dravidians (people who live in South India and believed to have come from the Mediterranean), Western Brachycephals (mostly people of Western India) and the Nordic Aryans (believed to have come from Central Asia and the last ones to arrive).

India has a variety of communities

India has had a long history of invasions and immigrations. Since ancient times, invaders have come specifically to plunder the country and then return back again for more plunders. Fallen for the charm of the land, some have stayed behind and married the locals. Some communities have come to India to seek refuge. You think of a religious community and you will find them in India. Due to India's strategic location and due to the fact that it is surrounded by water on three sides, the country also experienced trade with other countries for centuries. All these experiences added to the incredible richness of the country.

India is also very much a layered country in terms of cultural traditions. A section of Indian society lives in urban areas while the rest lives in the villages. Some Indians receive Western education while others receive traditional education and follow their traditional community beliefs. Some communities, particularly the tribal people of India especially in the rural or remote places are illiterate but have rich cultural heritage and following oral traditions. Some historians believe that they were the first inhabitants of India. India is a very fascinating country where people of many different communities and religions live together as a country.

Variety of languages

The Indian people speak a variety of languages. The Indian languages are divided into two major categories namely the Indo-Aryan languages of which about 75% of Indians speak and the Dravidian languages spoken by about 24% of the population. The rest speak languages belonging to the Austroasiatic and Tibeto-Burman languages.

But for convenience, the country recognizes one main language - the Hindi language. Hindi has been recognized as the official language in the constitution of India. While quite a lot of people do know English well, knowing a little bit of Hindi can be helpful in dealing with locals and those who you will interact the most such as taxi drivers, waiters, shop-keepers, hotel bell-boys, porters and so on.

Whenever you visit a country, learning a bit of its language is one of the best things you can do as a traveler. A few Hindi basic words to guide your direction is 'seedha' which means 'straight', 'nahi' which means 'No', accha or haa' meaning 'yes', and so on. Make sure you have a traveler's guide to Hindi at hand when you travel especially in the Northern part of the country. I have included some basic Hindi words in this book.

Variety of religious beliefs

Four major world religions originated in India namely Hinduism, Sikhism, Buddhism and Jainism. Buddhism and Jainism were off-shoots of Hinduism but developed their own structures and belief systems, becoming independent religions later. Islam, Christianity and Zoroastrianism are a few other religious belief systems in India. People with these different beliefs and cultural practices live harmoniously which has been the usual practice for centuries. This is why you find a variety of religious structures in India including temples (mandirs), mosques (masjids), churches (girja ghars), gurdwaras (Sikh temples) and even synagogues. Interestingly, there's a community in Eastern India called the 'Bene Israel' that claims to be the descendents of the lost Jewish tribe.

Variety of cultural customs and traditions

When you visit India, you will realize that Indians have many different kinds of traditions and customs. For example, in many Indian homes (though not all), it is customary to remove your shoes near the main entrance either inside or outside before you step into the room. If you do happen to be going to an Indian home, it might be polite to ask your host if you need to remove your shoes. Temples and mosques that are open to visitors also require you to take your shoes off and some of the larger and traditional places have places marked for visitors to keep their shoes. In religious places, like gurdwaras (a place of worship for the Sikhs) both men and women have to cover their heads. A traditional greeting among Indian Hindus is 'Namaste' in which both palms are joined and folded.

Variety of political practices

Just like different religions, India also has diverse political beliefs. There are a few pan-India political parties, as well as many regional parties pushing for the development and growth of a particular Indian state. There are parties with a slight militant streak to those with pacifist and democratic goals - the diversity in this as in other things in India is quite fascinating. Usually, except for 'bandhs' (close-down) called by a political party in which commercial activities comes to a stand-still in a particular place, you won't be affected as a traveler.

In terms of diversity, India is unmatched and some of the bad stories you hear about India will most probably be true but many will fade away when you come to India. If you are thinking of travelling to India, here's a simple suggestion – just leave all your previous notions about India behind and simply soak in the experience the country has to offer.

Indian food

Indian food is one of most liked food in the planet. No matter where you go in the world, you are bound to find an Indian restaurant. Unfortunately, many of these restaurants may not be serving the range and variety of cuisines that India has to offer. You will find that food varies from region to region in India. In addition; immigration, foreign invasions, trade, settlements and colonialism all have contributed to the kind of food India eats. In fact, every Indian state will have a specialty and is very much influenced by religion and culture. Remember many Indians are vegetarians but significant portion of the Indian people do eat meat. Eating of Beef is forbidden in the Hindu religion and it will be difficult for you to get hold of pork on the menu.

Some of the most popular Indian dishes include chicken tikka masala, butter chicken, matar paneer (made of Indian cheese and pees), chaat (a street food), malai kofta (creamed vegetarian meat balls) samosas (snacks), Indian styled chow mein, vegetable cutlets and naan bread. This is just a sample of what's popular but you will find a variety of dishes to cater for your taste buds.

About this book

This book is for those considering taking a tour to India or those who will be visiting India in the near future. The book deals with most of the common problems faced by tourists to India and contain everything they will need to know about the country as far as travel is concerned.

2. Best time to visit India

India is a big country so the fact is that there is no best time to visit this country. The Tropic of Cancer cuts right through the middle giving India a sub-tropical climate. Anytime can be a good time depending on which part of the country you are travelling to and what you want to experience. Generally, the country is said to be hot but the truth is that temperatures usually vary in different regions according to the season and the elevation from sea level.

Broadly, the country has three main seasons. A very hot and dry summer continues from mid-April to June. The south-west monsoon hit most parts of the country around mid-June and lingers till September bringing the rainy season. Once the rains clear up, the weather gets a little cooler and dry. There is hardly any snow except in the higher elevations in the winter months like in the upper regions of the Himalayas.

Northern India

Summer is exceptionally hot where the drier places have great extremes of day and night temperatures. In winters, temperatures can get close to or below freezing point and often there are cold waves. Between winter and summer, there is the brief lull of spring from February to March. The blossoms set the countryside on fire and you can catch this in action on a Northern India spring time tour. You can also experience the festival of Holi, the great Indian seasonal festival of colors that comes in 'Vasant' (March) or spring and enjoy many musical concerts and performances. If you are travelling to the desert regions of Rajasthan or Gujarat, the cool and dry time right just before winter is best for visits.

South-Western India

The Western region of India especially the area close to the Western Ghats gets considerable amount of rain, so you can catch the magical action of the Indian monsoons in this region. The south-west monsoon winds pick up moisture from the Arabian Sea and travel across the country bringing in rain. They hit the Himalayas in the upper north and begin their return journey along the same route around October which means that the Western Ghats receive two big spells of rain. From June-September and again in October, you can enjoy the beauty of the rich vegetation of the rain-soaked Western Ghats with dense rolling fog that adds mystique to the scene.

Southern India

Although the weather remains hot all round the year in these parts, the coastal regions are usually pleasant. You can enjoy the beaches at any time of the year except perhaps the very rainy season. The cooler season from October to

February has temperatures averaging 25 degree Celsius, making it their peak tourist season. Different places in Southern India have their own seasonal festivals, such as Onam in Kerala with its snake-boat races in mid-winter.

Eastern India

Like other parts of India, this region also has the regular monsoons with hot and cool seasons. You can time your visit to coincide with the long festival season starting around September and going on till November and December. In West Bengal and many parts of Eastern India, Durga Puja with colorful makeshift "pandals" (stages) and glittering idols turns streets into carnival like zones for about five days around the months of September or October. Other important festivals celebrated here and elsewhere in India include Diwali just a few weeks just after the Durga Puja celebrations.

North-Eastern India

This region experiences both the south-west monsoons and the north-eastern monsoons. From October to February, this region often experiences cyclones some of which cause huge destruction. You will need to check the weather before you travel in this region. If the rains are mild, you can enjoy viewing the rains generally from June to October. During the months of December and January there is a lot of music and nature related festivals in this area of India.

To experience the spirit of India, you have to be in the country during its festivals. Around mid-October or November, Diwali is celebrated with lights and firecrackers in most part of India especially the Northern plains. Holi is a spring festival, and various regions of India have their traditional harvest festivals around the end of winter. Onam is Kerala's harvest festival celebrated with a traditional long snake-boat competition. Goa is great to visit at different times particularly during the annual Goa Tourism Festival.

Come and enjoy the changing seasons of India and experience its vivid and vibrant celebrations – all year round! Although there is no best time to visit India, you will enjoy India during the months of November to end of March when the climate is cooler.

3. Geography of India

India is a country located in South Asia. It borders China, Nepal and Bhutan to the north and north-east; Bangladesh and Burma to the east and Pakistan to the west. The Arabian Sea, Bay of Bengal and the Indian Ocean marks the western, eastern and southern boundaries of the country respectively. India is the seventh largest country in the world by land area. It's is a peninsula which comprises of twenty-nine states and seven union territories. The country is blessed with a warm climate. And with over a billion people, it is the second most populous country in the world.

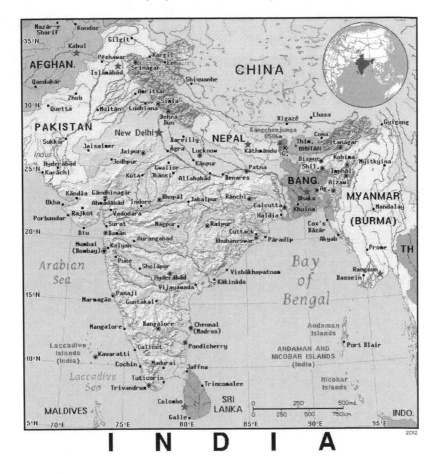

INDIA

Geography

Located in the northern hemisphere, India comprises of 2.2% of the world's landmass. That translates into 3.3 million square kilometers. Oceans in the south separate it from Africa, Indonesia and Australia. The Himalayas in the north keep the region separate from China and the rest of East Asia. There are mountain passes in the west, which foreigners have used throughout history to invade the lush, fertile and wealthy northern plains of the country.

Topography

The country shows a rich variety in topography. The northern plains are the most fertile in the country. The main rivers are Ganges and Brahmaputra that flow through these plains. The southern parts sit on a piece of hard rock known as Gondwanaland. There are mountain areas in the extreme north and north-east, while the Thar Desert occupies a large chunk of area in the west. The Andaman and Nicobar islands are at least a thousand kilometers from the mainland. A few of these islands are home to tribes that are still living like those from the stone or iron ages.

Population

Data from the genome project suggests that India is the second oldest continuously inhabited place in the world after Africa. Archaeological evidence shows an advanced civilization used to inhabit the place more than four millennia ago. There have been many migrations into the country making India the second most genetically diverse region on the earth after Africa. There are currently more than 1.2 billion people living in the country. Three-quarters of the population is Hindu while Islam is the second most popular religion. A little less than two-fifth of Indians are Muslims.

Climate

India has a warm climate. Tropic of Cancer passes right through the middle of the country. Seasonal rains called the monsoon have a big influence on the climate. The southern regions have a tropical, humid climate, while far in the north you are bound to encounter some of the coldest regions on earth. The eastern parts receive a lot of rain, at the same time there is a vast desert in the west. The plains have four seasons: summer, monsoons, post-monsoon (autumn) and winter.

Natural disasters

The state of West Bengal and the surrounding regions are prone to storms during the summers. The coastal regions were badly hit by the 2004 Asian tsunami. There was a devastating earthquake in Gujarat in 2001. Nonetheless the country is relatively immune to storms and earthquakes while flood and droughts being the most common natural disasters.

4. Places to visit in Eastern India

Featuring the sea, unspoiled hilly landscapes, ancient brick carvings, million years old rock formations and hidden wonders, Eastern India has eclectic attractions. Eastern India consists of the states of Odisha, Bihar, Chhatisgarh, Jharkhand, West Bengal and Sikkim.

Here are a few interesting places in this region

Odisha

Top attractions include the intricately layered 13th century India's oldest Sun Temple Konark Sun Temple and the Lingaraja Temple in Bhubaneshwar in the state capital along with ancient Buddhist pilgrimage sites of Udaygiri, Khandagiri, Lalitagiri and Ratnagiri. Puri is famous both for its sea and the ancient Jagannath temple. Bhitarkanika Bird Sanctuary and Mayurbhanj are popular with nature lovers. At Lake Chilka, Asia's largest saltwater lake, the Dolphin Point for dolphin sightings is also famous. Pipli a village about 35km from Puri is famous for its handicraft that showcases Odisha's rich artistic traditions.

Bihar

Associated with the growth of Buddhist and Jain religions, Bihar has many sacred monuments and sites. Nalanda is where there was an ancient international university and a rich Buddhist culture is a famous attraction in this state. The hill town of Rajgir, Vaishali, and Bodhgaya with the Mahabodhi Temple are renowned as ancient sites for Buddhist scholars and monks. Jal Mandir Jain Temple in Pawapuri is a white marble temple surrounded by a lotus lake and the Sher Shah Suri tomb in Sasaram are worth visiting.

Jharkhand

The state capital, Ranchi with the Hudroo Falls and the Ranchi Hills nearby, Hazaribagh and Jamsdhedpur with the Subarnarekha River and the Dalma Hills nearby are some top scenic hotspots. Baidyanath Dham is also an ancient religious destination popular amongst the locals.

Chhatisgarh

The horseshoe-shaped Chitrakote Falls, the Indravati Park with the tiger reserve are a few prominent attractions. Other hotspots include the culturally rich tribal district of Bastar, the centuries-old Kankar town and Bhoramdeo temple with intricate, erotic carvings.

West Bengal

The graceful Victoria Memorial, the bustling Dalhousie Square and Sudder Street, Nakhoda Masjid, Belur and Dakkhineshwar and the Portuguese-built Bandel Church give the state capital Kolkata and its surroundings a unique identity. Other West Bengal attractions include Darjeeling hill station, Bishnupur terracotta temples, the Mayapur ISCKON temple, the ancient mosques of Murshidabad and Maldah, and the Sunderbans mangroves (a bio-diverse region which West Bengal shares with India's neighbor Bangladesh). Purulia and Bankura have dense and culturally complex tribal settlements, hard, rocky terrain and centuries-old rock formations and valleys which are ideal for ecotourism and rock-climbing.

Sikkim

The many attractions of this mountainous small state include Chhangu Lake near the state capital Gangtok. Other sites include Tsomgo Lake, Guru-Dongmar Lake and the Rumtek Monastery. Pelling Town is a small town in West Sikkim where the Himalayas and the Kanchenjunga mountain ranges can be seen. Yuksom is often the base camp for those climbing the Kanchenjunga, the world's third highest peak. The picturesque Nathula Pass in the Indo-China corridor needs special permission to visit.

The 'Seven Sisters', the name given to the northeastern states of Meghalaya, Assam, Manipur, Mizoram, Arunachal Pradesh, Tripura and Nagaland are renowned for their natural beauty and ancient tribal cultures.

Here's what these northeastern states of India has to offer

Meghalaya

Near the hill station and state capital Shillong, scenic beauty abounds. The lush hills of Cherrapunji once recorded the world's highest rainfall. Mawllynong is another attractive destination.

Assam

The Kamakhya Temple in the Nilachal Hills and Madan Kamdeva Temple are ancient religious spots. The Manas Wildlife Sanctuary, Tezpur along the Brahmaputra River and the Halflong hill station are famous natural attractions.

Manipur

Loktak Lake, Sendrai Island, Singda Park and Sekta Archaeological Museum are top attractions. Keibul Lamjao National Park, Khongjom, Moreh and Manipur Zoological Garden showcase the rich biodiversity of this region.

Mizoram

Aizawl the state capital and Chamhai are important cities. The state has many wildlife sanctuaries such as Lengteng, Murlen, Chin Park, Phawngpui and the mountainous terrain also offer opportunities for ecotourism, camping, trekking and hiking adventures.

Arunachal Pradesh

This archaeologically rich state has many attractive places that are known for its fabulous orchids. The region has one of Asia's biggest orchidariums (a botanical garden dedicated to orchids). Namdapha National Park, Itanagar, Miao, Roing and Tawang are just a few attractions of this state.

Tripura

Ambasa and Kailashahar are top tourist attractions while the sculptures of Unakoti and the Kunjabon Palace testify to a rich cultural history. Trishna sanctuary and Rudrasagar Lake are popular among nature lovers.

Nagaland

The Intanki National Park, Mount Saramati and the culturally rich Zunheboto region are a few attractions in this state. The annual Hornbill Festival in December showcasing the Naga tribal diversity draws many international tourists.

5. Places to visit in Northern India

With the Himalayas standing like a wall on one side and the vast Thar Desert on the other with wide expanses of the fertile Northern plains running much of its length - North India is a tourist's delight. The states that make up Northern India are Jammu and Kashmir, Punjab, Haryana, Delhi, Uttarakhand and Uttar Pradesh.

A rich and ancient history, with the rise and fall of kingdoms right up to modern times, coupled with a well-developed tourism industry, enhances the appeal of this part of India.

Here is a look at the top North India's sightseeing spots

Jammu and Kashmir

Serenaded since ancient times for its vast mountains and princely gardens, the northernmost state lying in the Greater Himalayas has its special charm despite a troubled political history. The Dal Lake in Srinagar with the houseboats floating calmly in the tranquil waters with a backdrop of mountain peaks, Gulmarg with rose gardens blooming in the colder months and Pahelgaon are some of the top sightseeing spots. Some of these tourist spots have also been featured in many Bollywood movies. For Hindu pilgrims, Jammu's Vaishno Devi temple in the upper reaches of the Himalayas is also a top attraction.

Himachal Pradesh

Nestled in the Himalayas, this small state showcases a wealth of attractions like snowcapped mountains, fruit orchards and lush meadows with lilting mountain songs adding to the charm. Thronged by tourists, the hill stations of Shimla, Kulu and Manali look picture-perfect with graceful bungalows and other structures maintained since the British colonial era.

Punjab

The name of the state in the local language means the land of the five rivers. With a strong agricultural base and a highly prosperous local and overseas community, Punjab ranks among the wealthier states of India. A vibrant culture of dances and songs celebrates the rooted ethos of this state. The Sikh religion was born here and the Golden Temple in Amritsar is a top pilgrimage site for Sikhs and people of other communities from across India and beyond.

In the neighboring state of Haryana, the Karnal Lake on the west bank of the Yamuna in the centuries-old Karnal city attracts migratory birds and is a growing ecotourism destination.

Delhi

A city of many layers and built over and over throughout history, city of Delhi is a separate state in India. The capital of the Mughal Empire is also the capital of modern India and at the heart of its national politics and major administrative decisions. Filled with monuments dating back to the times of the Mughals and earlier, Old Delhi has most of the attractions like Red Fort, Purana Quilla, Jama Masjid, Humayun's Tomb etc. New Delhi is the newer area of the city with government buildings, offices, embassies and much else.

If you want to buy something then Delhi is a haven for shoppers. Janpath market in Delhi is very popular amongst foreign tourists. It is close to other shopping centers like the famous Connaught Place and the Palika Bazaar. Some of the best buys here include Pashmina Shawls and wool shawls and scarves from Kashmir, Indian clothes for women such as Kurtis and Churidars, brass ornaments and artifacts, carpets and other gift items are some of the many things you can buy. Mind you there are lots of hawkers and street vendors and if you did buy from them then you must take a look at some of the bargaining tips I have mentioned. Close to this place is the Raj Ghat, Mahatma Gandhi's memorial. This is great get away from the hustle and bustle of Delhi.

The top attractions of Delhi include Red Fort, India Gate, Jama Masjid, Qutab Minar, Lotus Bahai Temple, Humayun's Tomb, Lodhi Garden, Chandani Chowk (famous for food), Akshardham Hindu Temple and Connaught Place.

Uttar Pradesh

The largest state of India in terms of population, Uttar Pradesh literally means the northern land within the country. The northern plains with the River Ganges flowing through it make this part of India very fertile. Ancient civilizations rose and fell here. Varanasi also known as Banaras and Kashi is the oldest surviving city and the holiest city of the Hindus.

With its ghats (steps at a holy river), temples and g
of large numbers of devout worshippers the city is U
Pradesh's most visited place. Varanasi is very popular
amongst foreign tourists.

Haridwar is another important religious city, and the Har ke
Pauri Ghat shining with thousands of 'diyas' during the
evening "aarti" offers photo opportunities par excellence.

Agra is the site of the famous monument the Taj Mahal built
by Mughal Emperor Shah Jahan. The Taj Mahal is today one
of the World's Seven Wonders. The graceful monument of
love, built by Shah Jahan using Rajasthan's famous white
marble and precious stones from all over the world for the his
wife beloved Mumtaz Mahal is visited by tourists from across
the world. It is said that the world is divided into parts –those
who have seen the Taj Mahal and those who haven't.

Fatehpur Sikri containing vast ruins of empires is also
another top sightseeing destination near Delhi. Taj Mahal is
a must visit if you happen to be visiting Delhi. It's a day's trip
from Delhi and is easily reached by train, coach or taxi.

The temple town of Mathura is about 50 kilometers from
Agra and can be seen in a day. This is where Lord Krishna
was born. The most popular destination in Mathura is the
Keshav Dev Temple (or the Shri Krishna Janma Bhoomi).
Aurangzeb the despotic Mughal emperor had destroyed the
temple and built a mosque over it. The Hindus had to
compromise and build a temple next to the mosque. The
temple is very controversial as some Hindus want the
original temple and land back.

Rajasthan

The land of the rajas (kings) as the name suggests flows with
stories, colorful people and huge castles and forts. While it
lies more to the west than the north of India, in tourism
brochures it is considered as one arm of the Golden Triangle
for sightseers - the other two arms being Delhi and Agra.
Camel safari in the Thar Desert, tours of the 'Pink City' of
Jaipur, the Hawa Mahal in Jodhpur, Dilwara Temple on
Mount Abu are some of the few major attractions. It is said

[34]

that every third tourist coming to India from abroad also visit Rajasthan. Places to visit include palaces and forts of Jaipur, Jodhpur, Bikaner and Jaisalmer along with lakes of Udaipur. Mount Abu is a popular hill station and has many Jain temples of noteworthy importance. Pushkar holds one of the biggest cattle and camel fairs in the world around the months of October and November. If you are want to learn more about Indian culture then you must visit this fair. You will get to witness folk music and dances, strange magic shows, camel races and a range of Indian traditional entertainment and competitions.

Uttarakhand

Occupying the northern part of Uttar Pradesh and cradled in the Shivalik ranges, this small state beckons exciting adventure tourism opportunities. Nature lovers and adventure sports lovers enjoy white water rafting and other water sports in the fast-flowing rivers. Uttaranchal is also an important religious destination in India. It is said that the sage

Vyasa wrote the Hindu epic Mahabharata in this region. Some of the places to visit include Rishikesh, hill station of Mussoorie, holy city of Haridwar and famous hill station of Nainital. There are numerous national parks and wildlife sanctuaries in the state. The Valley of Flowers National Park which is a UNESCO World heritage site is also situated here.

6. Places to visit in Southern India

Cultures and kingdoms that go back centuries shape the history of South India making each of its regions distinctive with traditional art forms, dance and music expressions, literature, languages and much more. Lying south of the Tropic of Cancer, this part of India is known for its mostly hot weather, coastal places and ancient temples.

The states comprising South India are Tamil Nadu, Karnataka, Kerala, Seemandhra and Telengana. Each of these states, including Telangana and Seemandhra (the two states into which the big state of Andhra Pradesh has been carved) has a flavor unique unto itself which is what makes South Indian tours so interesting.

Check out some interesting places in South India

Tamil Nadu

This state is known for its cultural heritage and deep roots embodied in gorgeously carved ancient temples and local handicrafts. Madurai the temple city with the 40 centuries plus old Meenakshi temple in the temple city of Madurai, the Seven Pagodas of Mahabalipuram and the ancient

Rameshwaram temple on the island of Rameswaram are a few famous religious places. The green beauty of the hill stations of Yercaud, Kodaikanal and Ooty give them a romantic flavor. The Aurobindo Ashram in Pondhicherry attracts both national and international tourists. Down south, the Vivekananda Rocks in Kanyakumari forms the southernmost tip of India. This is also the place where waters of three different water bodies belonging to the Indian Ocean, the Arabian Sea and the Bay of Bengal meet. In the ancient times, Kanyakumari was a great centre for art and religion and an important trade and commerce centre. Some of the places to visit in Kanyakumari include the Kumari Amman or the Kanyakumari Temple, the statue of Tamil poet Thiruvalluvar, the Gandhi Memorial and of course the sea shore.

Karnataka

Mysore and Hampi are the important tourist attractions in this state. The Mysore Palace is centuries old, and contains a museum worth exploring. The annual Dussehra festival every autumn in Mysore see throngs of visitors as the celebrations continue in the form of grand elephant parades, fireworks and general merrymaking with the illuminated palace in the backdrop. In Hampi, the ruins of the once mighty Vijaynagar Empire are top attractions and with 500 plus monuments spread over miles, there are plenty of sites worth exploring. Fascinatingly centuries old shaped rock carvings and ruins make up the unique landscape in Hampi which is also considered a world heritage site. Close to the state capital Bengaluru (previously known as Bangalore), the wildlife sanctuary is also becoming popular with tourists. Coorg in the Western Ghats region is lush during the monsoons with its coffee plantations and mouth watering cuisine makes it very distinctive place in India.

Seemandhra

Vizag the post city with a longer traditional name Vishakhapatnam is a top port and tourist destination where visitors can enjoy viewing the sea in a hilly landscape. Araku Valley with its miles of green rolling meadows is an attractive location for honeymooners. The Borra Caves in the Araku Valley are natural limestone caves going back thousands of centuries. Tirupati Temple in the Tirumala Hills sees huge crowds of pilgrims every day. Nagarjunasagar Dam is another important attraction in this state. The museum on an island near the dam location gives an insight into the Nagarjuna Konda, a rich Buddhist centre of learning.

Telangana

The twin cities of Hyderabad and Secunderabad have fascinating newer and older layers have many interesting sights. The Nizam's Museum, and the Salar Jung Museum in Hyderabad entirely made up of antiques collected by Mir Yousuf Ali Khan Salar Jung III, is some of the few interesting places. Distinctive in the Hyderabad cityscape is the Char Minar built by the Nizam of Hyderabad and the ancient Golconda Fort. This region is famous for the world's most famous and coveted gems including the Hope Diamond and the Koh-i-Noor.

Kerala

The southernmost state of India is small but its distinctive landscape of quiet backwaters, coconut-fringed backdrops and traditional boats have given it the epithet 'God's Own Country'. Kochi has Fort Kochi, a popular attraction. The waterfront with its picturesque Chinese nets used by the local fishermen, gives the town a unique appearance.

Kerala's beaches, backwaters, mountain ranges and wildlife sanctuaries are some of the major attraction for tourists to the state. In addition, if you want to learn about or try out Ayurvedic treatment (relaxation and stress relief) then Kerala is a great to do it.

The Wayanad Wildlife Sanctuary is a famous ecotourism destination. The region also has the archaeologically rich

Edakkal Caves with its Stone Age carvings. The imposing sea-facing Bekal Fort in Kasaragord is Kerala's largest fort and St Francis Church originally built by the Portuguese in 1503 is India's oldest European church. Backwater trips in Vembanad, houseboat trips in Kumarakom and watching snake-boat races during Onam, Kerala's annual rice harvest festival in August, and traditional Ayurvedic massages in eco-resorts are some popular ways to enjoy the attractions of Kerala. Lake Periyar, Lake Munnar, Varkala Beach and the city of Trivandrum are some of the other popular attractions in Kerala.

7. Places to visit in Western India

The western part of India beckons tourists with its many interesting opportunities for sightseeing and ecotourism activities. The lush evergreen Western Ghat region bordering the coast and overlooking the Arabian Sea makes Western India a treasure-trove for nature lovers. This part of India has many industrialized states with many urban centers adding to its commercial importance.

The major states of Western India are Maharashtra, Gujarat and Goa along with two Union Territories Daman and Diu, and Dadra and Nagar Haveli. The Western Ghats region is full of numerous hill stations which were established during colonial times. The Western Ghats region has recently been declared a UNESCO World Heritage region, and it holds much ecological importance.

Take a look at some top places to sightsee in Western India

Maharashtra

Literally meaning 'great state', Maharashtra has many important cities like Pune, Nasik, Mumbai, and Nagpur, each with its distinctive identity. Pune has a thriving student community and many educational institutes of national importance. Mumbai is India's commercial capital and the hub of the world famous Hindi language film industry termed Bollywood. A few noteworthy places to visit in this cosmopolitan and eclectic city are the beach areas in Juhu and Bandra, Colaba and the Marine Drive where the Taj Hotel is located, Powai Lake, Haji Ali Mosque, Banganga, an International Museum of Toilets, and the historic Elephanta Caves.

A few hours' drive away from Mumbai as the base, Western Ghat hill stations of Khandala, Mahabaleshwar, Matheran and Lonavala are famous for their green beauty during the monsoons. Matheran is another hill station that has many attractions like Rambagh Vantage Point from which to see the beautiful panoramic surroundings.

Goa

The tiny state of Goa, with its beaches, music, laidback lifestyle and gracious churches, is a major tourist destination. Its Portuguese heritage mixes with the culture of the local fishing community to create a vibrant adventure for local and international tourists. Braganza Pereira Mansion, Salim Ali Bird Sanctuary, Dudhsagar Falls and Panjim are top places to visit.

The state and its surroundings have numerous gothic churches and chapels with interesting histories. Many churches are decorated for important Catholic festivals and also feature colorful and grand parades. The annual Goa Carnival held before Easter Sunday and the November International Goa Film Festival among other festivals that keeps the atmosphere vibrant in Goa.

Gujarat

A state with a wealth of natural resources, tribal communities, industries and urban centers Gujarat is of major significance for business and commerce. Ahmedabad, the largest city of Gujarat has a layered history and situated on the banks of the Sabarmati River. The Ashram of Mohandas Karamchand Gandhi is popular amongst visitors to the city. Other attractions in Ahmedabad include Sidi Sayid Mosque, Adalaj step-well (a unique water building), Teen Darwaja, Jama Masjid, Kite Museum, Calico Textiles Museum, Shreyas Folk Museum, Vintage Car Museum and Kankaria Lake.

Elsewhere in Gujarat, top places to visit are Vadodara, Jamnagar and Porbander (where M.K Gandhi was born). Another interesting place in Gujarat is Patan, the location of an ancient city where once there was a thriving Buddhist culture. Gir Forest Sanctuary is known for its population of lions and other wild animals. Kutch is known for many wildlife sanctuaries such as the 'Kutch desert wildlife sanctuary' in the Great Rann of Kutch where flamingoes congregate to breed.

Dadra and Nagar Haveli

Tucked between the big states of Maharashtra and Gujarat, this Union Territory has its own share of attractions. Vanganga Lake and Silvassa Tribal Museum are worth visiting here and the proximity to the Western Ghats also makes it an interesting wildlife tourism destination. The coastal boundaries of this tiny place are a rich ecological site with the saltpans on the northern coast and the beaches on the southern coast harboring various kinds of wildlife. The south coast also has limestone cliffs that add to its picturesque appeal.

Daman and Diu

Featuring gentle beaches and clean coastland, this Union Territory of India (ruled directly by the central government) has been renowned for its beauty since ancient times. The Fort of Diu overlooking the sea is a top attraction here and the Basilica of Bom Jesus is also frequented by many visitors. A 16th century fort, the Moti Daman Fort of a Portuguese lineage is another important attraction. Jampore and Nagoa are a few famous beaches in Diu.

8. Culture of India

The culture of India can be traced back to thousands of years. The lifestyle, languages, ceremonies, religions, beliefs, customs, traditions, arts and values all form the basis for recognizing Indian culture. Not only is Indian culture unique but it is also diverse. The country is peculiar in a way as it does not share the same culture throughout the country. Every state or region in India celebrates the existence of its own different culture which may be differ to more or less extent from one part of the country to another.

The sense of dressing, the food habits, even religion, art forms, music and languages all vary from region to region. Broadly India can be divided as North India, East India, West India, South India and North-Eastern part of India. Though this does not clearly differentiate the cultural diversity, it can still be used to get a bigger picture of the cultural differences of the country.

The population of each of the above categorized region shares some of the cultural values if not every aspect of it. For example: South Indian food is somewhat similar in all the four states namely Karnataka, Tamil-Nadu, Andhra-Pradesh and Kerala; they all hail from the original Dravidian race; they mostly celebrate same festivals with a little customization in the way they celebrate them. Similarly, many states of North India would have more or less similar culture.

While this was talking about the diversity in Indian culture, there is a lot more to it. Yes, India gives true meaning to "Unity in Diversity". Even with such diverse cultural beliefs, people in India follow the same rich culture that is common throughout the country. India comes together to celebrate many festivals that are celebrated throughout India such as Holi, Diwali, Dussera and other National festivals.

The official language Hindi is spoken all throughout the country and the national dress sari is adorned by one and all. The cultural heritage of India is preserved by every Indian national who takes pride in saying 'I am Indian'.

If you like dressing up and if you want to see the beauty accessories, makeup and clothing of the world then you ought to visit India. Saris, chudi dhars, lehengas, sararas, sherwanis and dhothis are the cultural extravaganza that you can find only in India. Indian clothing is just as unique as its religious beliefs. The traditional Jeweler men and women wear are par excellence of craftsmanship which cannot be done with words. The jumkas (special earrings), payals (anklets), the bindi (worn on head to decorate forehead), the kadas (anklets and bracelets mostly worn by men), are something which cannot be found elsewhere in the world.

India is the land where kings have ruled for ages. The customs and traditions that have been left behind and monuments they have built have given India a rich cultural heritage. The enigma of the majestic Indian monuments like Taj Mahal is a must to behold in one's life time and can be considered as the national monument that every Indian takes pride in.

The dance forms such as Gaudiya Nritya, Prakriti Ora, Mohiniyattam, Odissi, Kathakali, Kuchipudi, Manipuri dance, Bharata Natyam and Kathak are the traditional Indian forms of dance which add value to enrich the culture.

Indian cuisine is yet another example of the uniqueness of Indian culture. The varieties of food you find in India are truly amazing. From starters to main course to desserts and drinks the combination of ingredients and the method of cooking in every dish are just out of imagination for any layman of Indian culture. Pani puri, chaats, chatnies, paneer makahanwala, dosa, idli, samosa, biryani, gajar ka halwa, rosagolla, butter chicken, lassi....the list is just the beginning. Even if I write a few pages with just the names of the dishes I would be able to complete just 5% of the varieties. The spices of India is famous world over.

Marriages in India are often a big deal and involve a big fat wedding which goes beyond the economical status of the two parties. It is more of an arranged marriage but slowly is making a shift with love marriages being the choice of today's youngsters.

India is where religions of Hinduism, Buddhism, Jainism and Sikhism also known as the Eastern Religions (Indian religions) came into being. Indian temples like Sun Temple and Birla Mandir or temples in South India are the master pieces of architecture and the art of stone carving. There are hundreds of Gods and Goddesses worshiped in this holy land. Religions, castes and sub-castes are the hierarchy of social division which was formed and followed from thousands of years ago based on the kind of job people did. This is also the base for the Indian people who choose to worship different Gods depending on their caste and tradition.

Unfortunately, the culture of India does suppress women making them the weaker sections of the society. Community violence and castism sometimes become the reason for intolerance in Indian society. Though a lot has changed and a lot more will change with time, a section of the society in India will always lag behind to some extent or the other.

All said - the culture of India is definitely a matter of pride for every Indian and something to be watched and explored by the world.

9. Things you should bring to India

Although you can buy or get most things done in India but to make it a hassle free trip ideally you should bring a few things.

Here's a list of things you should bring to India

Photocopies of your passport

Hotel staff will ask you to take a look at your passport and they will even photocopy it. Perhaps you can offer photocopies instead. Also just in case, you lose your passport, it might be a good idea to keep some photocopies of your passport. You might consider sending a scanned copy of your passport and tickets to yourself by email just in case you lose your photocopies too.

Toilet paper

Although most good hotels will have toilet paper in their bathrooms, however budget hotels will not have them. And in many remote or even smaller towns in India, it will be difficult to get hold of toilet paper. It might be useful if you take a few rolls of toilet paper till you find a shop where you can buy them. This will keep you going for the first few days of your arrival.

Mosquito repellents

Mosquitoes are a menace in India and no matter where you go, there will be mosquitoes around. Just buy some mosquitoes repellents in the form of mosquito bands, sprays or cream to prevent them from biting you.

Basic medication

Although medicines can be found everywhere in India, it's a good idea to take some over the counter medication such as paracetamol, aspirin, Imodium and other over the counter medication you are likely to use.

Travel pouches to hide your money

You can find good travel pouches on Amazon or EBay to hide your money and passport under your belt. You can easily hide your valuables and keep them safe from pickpockets. Pickpockets are everywhere in India specially in crowded places such as bazaars, open markets, railway stations, religious places and so on. You must hide money and other valuables and secret travel pouches do the job well.

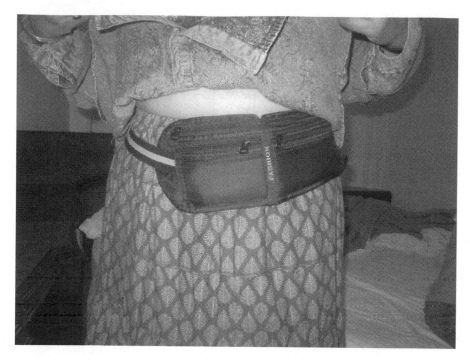

Travel adapter

The electricity supplied in India is at 440 volts at 50 Hz. You will need to carry plugs that have three round pins in a triangular pattern to fit in the wall sockets.

Camera

India is very photogenic place and you should not come to India without a camera. Make sure your camera is of good quality so that you can capture your moments in India. There are so many things that you can take photos of. Don't forget it! I bet you will take so many photos that you will run out of memory – bring an extra memory card.

Hindi travel phrase book

You should learn some basic Hindi even though English is widely spoken in India. I have written a book called, "Essential Hindi Words And Phrases For Travelers To India" and is available in Amazon (ISBN-10: 1492752517).

[55]

Alternatively, you can learn some Hindi words and phrases on my website ShaluSharma.com and even listen to me speak it out. I have compiled a list of common Hindi words and phrases in the chapter "Common Hindi words and phrases" in this book. Even if you learn a few words, it can go a long way.

Mobile phone

Don't forget to bring your mobile phone with you and make sure you activate roaming. You can also bring an unlocked handset and buy a SIM card at the airport.

Basic first aid kit

Although most sensible travelers buy travel insurance but if something did happen in India, there are many doctors around. You hotel should able to able to direct you to a doctor. But nonetheless, you must bring a basic first aid kit with you. A very basic one would do nicely.

Antibacterial wipes

India is a dirty and dusty place. You might consider bringing some antibacterial wipes or foam with you. This can be particularly handy if you are travelling with children. It's a good idea to use it before eating food at restaurants in India.

Sunscreen

India is hot place so don't forget to bring high quality sunscreen with sun protection factor of 50.

Sunglasses

You should consider wearing sunglasses to keep the intense rays of the sun out of your eyes especially if you are travelling in the summer months.

Travel locks

Hand luggage is often kept unlocked by tourists but it's a good idea to keep it locked just in case someone slides a hand in it and steal your valuables. A basic lock which can be locked and unlocked quickly is a good idea.

Comfortable clothing

Make sure your clothes are comfortable to wear. Cotton clothes are ideal in climates such as that of India. India can be hot in the summer and cold in the winter. So light cotton clothes for the summer and warm clothes for the winter is a must. If you are travelling during the monsoons, a rain coat is a must.

Tampons

Tampons in India can be difficult to get hold of as most women in India use sanitary pads. In fact, women in the villages still use pieces of cloth although sanitary pads are now available cheaply in various parts of India. So if you use tampons, you must bring some of these with you.

Handkerchief

India being a hot country, you are going to sweat so a handkerchief is a good idea to carry with you. Tissues will do the trick but they are not really ideal in a hot climate. With handkerchiefs, you can wash and dry overnight and it's ready to use the next day.

Cap or hat

Caps can keep the sun of you head and face. I always make my children wear the cap in the heat. A baseball cap would do nicely.

Credit Cards

There are lots of ATM machines for you to take cash out. In addition, most shops are now accepting credit cards so bring your credit card with you as it's much safe to use them compared to your debit cards.

Antiperspirant

You might not be able to find roll-on antiperspirants but you can find other types quite easily. Mind you, India is one hot place and you might wish to take a can of antiperspirant with you if you sweat like a fish.

Female Urinary Devices

Female urination devices (FUD) are urination aids that allow women to urinate while standing. They are quite cheap and you could bring a few just in case you don't like some of the dirty public toilets. Although not an important item, you never know it just might come in handy. Mind you, Indian public toilets are dirty. You can read more about it on my website here http://www.shalusharma.com/female-urination-devices-for-your-travels-to-india/.

10. Vaccinations for India

India is a tropical country and most governments of the world advice their citizens to take precautions before going to India. But before taking any vaccinations make sure you are update with your routine vaccinations such as measles-mumps-rubella (MMR) vaccine, diphtheria-tetanus-pertussis vaccine, chickenpox vaccine, polio and your yearly flu jabs (if you do take them). Since diphtheria, tetanus and polio are risks in India and many other countries, it is important that you talk to your doctor about these vaccinations.

Let's take a look at some of the jabs you must take before you come to India

Hepatitis A

Hepatitis A is a liver disease spread by contaminated food and water. Unfortunately, Hepatitis A is common in India and other developing countries. Therefore you might consider taking the vaccination for Hepatitis A before coming to India. In addition, the best way to avoid it is by not drinking tap water, food from street vendors, by not eating raw eggs and unwashed fruits and vegetables. Make sure you wash your hands before you eat food in India. It is recommended that you take the Hepatitis A vaccination two weeks before travel.

Typhoid

Again typhoid fever is a disease that is spread by contaminated food and water. It is common in a country like India. Precaution methods are the same as that of Hepatitis A. You might be advised by your family doctor to take this vaccination before you come to India. It is recommended that you take the typhoid vaccination two weeks before travel.

Malaria

Malaria is a disease that spreads through mosquito bites and malaria in India is rampant. Delhi in particularly is notorious for its mosquito related diseases such as malaria and dengue-fever. You must take precautions before coming to India. Although there are no vaccinations for malaria, there are prescription medicines that will allow you to prevent malaria which you will need to take before, during, and after your trip. One way is take some mosquito repellents that contain DEET (the active ingredient that repels insects), mosquito bands or nets. You must wear full sleeved clothes during the monsoons as this is the time when mosquitoes breed in large numbers. You can also buy products like "AllOut" or creams such as "Odomus" in India that will prevent mosquitoes from coming near you.

Japanese Encephalitis

Japanese encephalitis is a viral infection of the brain that spreads through mosquito bites. India is one of those countries where there is an increased risk of Japanese Encephalitis. A course of the vaccine will give you 98% protection against it. This vaccination is particularly important if you are planning to visit India during monsoons and if you are visiting for a longer duration. It is recommended that you take this vaccination one month before travelling.

Rabies

Rabies is spread by the saliva of stray dogs, bats, monkeys and other mammals in India. Unfortunately, there are lots of these stray dogs. There is a significant stray population of monkeys in many cities of India in including Delhi and Agra (where the Taj Mahal is situated). Children are particularly likely to play with dogs and if they were to get licks from infected dogs than chances are that it will be passed on. Those with children and those who might be doing a lot of out-door activities such as trekking, camping or engaging in wild-life activities then it might be good idea to consider rabies vaccination. It is recommended that you take the rabies vaccination one month before travel.

Cholera vaccination

Again cholera is spread by contaminated water and food and is common in India. If you are travelling in the rainy season than it is recommended that you take the cholera vaccination. It is recommended that you take it at least two weeks before you travel to India.

Please note: You must talk to your doctor or your travel nurse before coming to India and get professional medical advice.

11. How to deal with the heat?

India has a reputation for its intense heat and the bright white-hot Indian sun is legendary. For travelers especially those who come from cooler climates, the Indian heat can be overwhelming. But with some protection and planning, you can avoid the worst of the heat in India.

Here are some ways to beat the Indian heat

Wear light clothes

Stick to lightweight loose-fitting fabrics that you can breathe in. Heavyweight fabrics or those that cling to your skin are definitely a no-no. Wear lightweight open-toed sandals to keep your feet cool and comfortable. Shaded glasses, anti-glare glasses and sunglasses and suchlike are ideal to protect your eyes from the sun. Cover your head with cloth or wear a cap when you go out in the daytime. Buy a few lightweight handheld fans; you find them being sold sometimes by the roadside usually made of plastic or natural materials. Fan yourself with these to cope with the heat.

Think wet

Carry wet tissues and wipe your face from time to time, to remove the grime and feel cooler. Wherever you can, stop at roadsides and splash your face with water. You can also have light scarves or cotton towels with you to cover your arms from the heat and dust especially in speeding autos or cycle rickshaws. If you feel too hot, simply soak the cloth in water from a roadside tap and cool your face and arms. You can also use wet towels to wrap around your head in very hot weather. The sun will cause this to dry up in no time.

Eat light

To stay cool in the heat, eat light and try to avoid spices as much as you can in your meals. Fresh fruits are ideal (but wash them before you eat), especially those with a high water content like cucumber, guava, citrus fruits and water-melons. Drink plenty of fresh fruit juices and especially traditional juices like nimboo paani (lime juice), sugarcane juice and tender coconut water. These are cheap, plentifully available and work well to counter the heat.

Use anti-mosquito protection

The hot humid climate often causes mosquitoes to proliferate, so use mosquito nets or mosquito coils in hotels. You can also use creams like Odomos popular locally to keep the mosquitoes away.

Enjoy splashes

Swimming pools are great for beating the heat and if you can soak yourself in the water. If you stay in a hotel with a swimming pool, you can take a swim in the water and refresh yourself. Take plenty of showers during the day, especially once in the morning and once after you return from your sightseeing tour.

Hydration is the key

Drink plenty of water and stay hydrated. Carry fluids and solutions of salt, sugar and water when you travel. Perspiration causes a lot of water to drain out of the body, so you need to replenish that in order to avoid getting dehydrated or suffering sunstrokes. There are plenty of stalls on the road side where you can grab a soda or fizzy drinks.

Drink water or drinks at intervals

If you are travelling to India in the summer then temperatures are going to be very high. In places like Delhi, it can reach up to 45 degree Celsius. You will need to keep drinking at regular intervals. Either carry your own drinks or bottled water with you or buy them at shops whenever you can. Pepsi and Coke are widely available in India and relatively safe.

Protect your skin

The Indian sun can burn your skin and cause it to develop rashes unless you protect it well. Wear sunscreen with an SPF content of at least 40 or 50 because anything less than that will not suffice given India's hot and humid conditions. Apply a coating of sunscreen liberally on your face, arms and other uncovered areas of your body, half an hour before you go out. Keep the sunscreen lotion or cream with you handy inside your travel kit and apply from time to time all the time you are in the sun. You can also apply prickly heat talcum powder and antiperspirants to reduce perspiration.

Use waterproof cosmetics

Women are often in tough situations when it comes to dressing up in India. They tend to sweat quite a lot and sadly cosmetics get smudged even after it have been carefully applied. If you have to attend parties and need to wear

[67]

makeup, try using water-proof cosmetics that stay intact in the heat and humidity.

Plan strategically

Avoid going out too much during the noon time if you can especially if you are travelling with kids. Many Indians especially in rural areas use the hot afternoons to catch up on their sleep and you will find people enjoying an afternoon siesta even on the roadside in the shade. Use the early mornings and the evenings when the temperature cools a bit for most of your outings.

12. Guide to drinking water

Water is the route for many gastro-intestinal disorders in India. Chances are that you have heard of the word 'Delhi Belly'. Trust me, it does exist and if you do not take precautions then you might end up with it too. In majority of the cases, the infection occurs through the drinking water or the water that is used for cooking.

While you can stick to hygienic places for your food requirements, avoid dirty looking food or suspiciously watery dishes - what do you do about drinking water? India's tap water in most places is left untreated and even locals often do not use it for drinking. They may use it for activities like washing their faces or bodies, but if you do so, try not to let any water get into your mouth. You can boil the water during your stay in India and use it for drinking, especially if you have small kids with you. The other alternative that many tourists go for is to buy bottled water in India.

You will find that bottled water is being sold everywhere - in restaurants, shops, the roadside and railway platforms of India. Mind you, not all of them are equally safe therefore you must be careful what you drink.

Take a look at this guideline for choosing and buying drinking water in India

Choose well-known brands

Bottled water is very popular not only amongst the tourists but also locals as well. There are two types of bottled drinking water in India. They are classified as **'packaged water'** in which the water has been put through treatment processes to make it safe for drinking and then the other is the **'mineral water'** where the water is supposed to have come from natural underground sources which is then bottled.

Some traders are tricking the people! What they are doing is, putting tap water in plastic bottles, sticking a label on them and selling them on to people as packaged water. This is why it is a good idea to stick to well-known brands when you buy your drinking water in India. Some of the big brands that market mineral water in India include Bisleri which was the earliest to enter the Indian market. After Bisleri, the other big bottled water brands that came to India were Aquafina and Kinley. These are mostly available in the big cities or in stores attached to restaurants. One of the key reasons many tourists stick to the big brands for drinking water in India is because of the quality standard. With the local brands, you never know if the quality standards are enforced or not. So if you are in doubt, it is better to stick to popular and known brands. Remember these popular brands maybe be more expensive but it's better to be safe than sorry.

Check the seal

Sadly, India is a country where many kinds of dubious activities happen besides everything that's vibrant and beautiful so it's good to be on your guard. One of the common ways unscrupulous people cheat in case of drinking water is to open the seal of the bottle and replace the packaged water with regular water from the tap. Whenever you buy bottled water in India, it is always a good idea to check the seal. Usually if the seal is unbroken, it indicates that the bottle has not been tampered with and you can safely drink the water.

Most restaurants will ask if you want regular water or the mineral water. This generally means that the mineral water will be packaged bottles. Ask them what kind of mineral water they have and if they have a variety then ask them for the popular ones. Many restaurants now have water purifiers which supply decent water but nonetheless for safety's sake most tourists often go for mineral or packaged water.

Check the label

If you are buying a well-known brand of drinking water then always check the label. Companies always use the same kind of font and color scheme for their branding no matter which city you are travelling too. But there may be subtle differences if it's fake. Check for things like a miss-spelling, a slightly different font, a slight variation in name which you may overlook in a hurry and so on.

Avoid buying bottled water at railway stations

Usually a lot of fake packaged drinking water is sold at railway stations. This is where passengers are eager to quickly buy a bottle and stay hydrated on their journeys. If you can, then try to stay away from buying bottled water on railway stations. A good idea is to buy them before you come to the railway station. Not all of the shops on the railway platform will be selling fake packaged water – if a shop is busy then most likely that they are genuine. In Air Conditioned (AC) class railway compartments, the railways pantry car usually supplies bottled water with meals. This is included in the ticket cost and you can drink this water safely.

13. Avoiding water borne diseases

The humid and hot climate in many parts of India is a favorable breeding ground for many kinds of germs. The stagnant puddles that accumulate during the arrival of the monsoons contribute to the appropriate conditions for mosquitoes to thrive. Malaria and other mosquito-borne diseases like Japanese encephalitis or dengue are an ever-present reality in most parts of the country and sadly some of them can be fatal if care is not taken.

Here are some ways to deal with the risks of water borne diseases in India

Check your drinking water

One of the crucial questions that you need to deal on Indian tours is that of its water supply. Most of the tap water unless its water from a deep tube-well source is basically unfit for drinking purposes. While you find many taps by the roadside or at railway stations, you cannot always be sure that they are safe to drink. Some of the diseases you can acquire by drinking such water include gastroenteritis, amoebiosis, jaundice, typhoid and cholera. Simply – do not drink out of the tap.

As mentioned in the previous section, it is a good idea to buy and carry your own water supplies. You can get bottled water from the big brands like Kinley, Bisleri etc. as in many shops and restaurants. You can also try filtered water or water that has been processed through purifiers or you can boil the water before drinking especially if you have small kids with you. In restaurants, the waiter may ask if you want regular water or the mineral variety. If you are sure that the regular water comes via a water purifier, it may be okay to drink. But in most cases, stick to the safe course of paying a little more for bottled mineral water. Also, whichever bottled water brand you buy, check that the seal is intact and you are not being given tap-water in the guise of clean drinkable water. You may often find Indian travelers use Zeoline (anti-bacterial used in aquariums) and add it to the water they drink to make it drinkable. India has a thriving trade in counterfeit or spurious items so be careful.

Avoid food items with too much water

It is a good idea to keep away from food items that look too watery unless you know the source and that it has been prepared hygienically. It is also a good idea that you do not consume MILK. Many travelers to India who do not have the immunity often end up suffering traveler's dysentery, diarrhea and other water-borne diseases by consuming milk. As a rule, try to stay away from milk unless you are sure it has not been diluted with water. As for street food, travelers have different kinds of rules about this according to their appetite for adventure and risk. If you want to try street food, go for fried and fresh varieties. Avoid sauces, chutneys and other liquids that are often served as dips. In the same note, try to avoid fruit juices from the roadside. If you do try them, make sure then there is no water in the container where the juices have been squeezed. Also, avoid salads as it's not always possible to know about the quality of the water used for washing vegetables. Chances are that the water used is tap water which could well have been contaminated. You just have to be careful and ask a lot of questions to be sure what you are consuming. Be careful during the monsoons as most water-borne diseases occur during this time.

Take extra care during monsoons – India's rainy season

The monsoons are a great time to travel as everything turns lush green after the sweltering summer heat but it is also a time for epidemics and mass outbreaks of diseases. Most Indian roads, especially if they have pot-holes or un-tarred surfaces, turn into slushy puddles during the monsoons. If you were to step into the puddles by mistake then make sure to clean your feet thoroughly with antiseptic soap or lotion. Leptospirosis is another water-borne disease affecting humans in India. The bacteria that cause this disease can enter your body through nicks and cuts in the skin, the eyes, mouth, nose or vagina.

A good idea is to use the disinfectant Dettol liquid in your baths or bucket and taking a quick shower. Another option is Dettol soap which does the same thing. But do remember Dettol liquid can be toxic and you need to check if it suits you or not.

Wherever you stay, be sure that there is no stagnant water nearby which could breed mosquito larvae. Check for standing water in vases, buckets, bathtubs, flower pots etc.

Whilst these are some basic precautions to follow, make sure to have taken the regular vaccinations as per your doctor's advice before coming to India. Also, pack anti-malarial repellents in your medical kit and stay safe and keep your eyes open regarding water-borne diseases during your tour of India.

14. How to keep off mosquitoes?

Mosquitoes are an ever-present menace in most parts of India. Mosquitoes not only cause angry bites but they are also carriers of dreaded diseases like malaria, dengue, Japanese encephalitis, chikungunya and so on. So, you have every reason to be wary. But there are ways that you can protect yourself. Here are some ways to keep them away as the locals do and with some common sense you will be able keep these dreaded mosquitoes at bay.

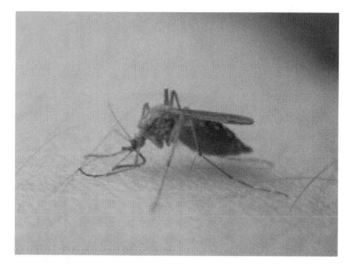

Mosquito-repellant creams

Buy creams that you can apply all over your body to keep mosquitoes off. Keep applying the cream regularly as the sweat released from the body makes the action of these creams fade away over time. Citronella oil-based creams are usually safe for most skin types and you can safely apply it on an infant's skin too. Ask for natural mosquito repellants when you go to a local store.

Mosquito nets

If your hotel room is air-conditioned then you do not need to worry. But if it is not, make sure to have mosquito nets at night. For safety's sake, it is a good idea to carry your own mosquito nets. That way you can set these up to enjoy peaceful nights free from annoying mosquito buzzes even if your hotel does not provide for them. Most medium-range hotels in India do provide mosquito nets though. Make sure the nets are well-tucked on all sides.

Mosquito coils

Another effective remedy is mosquito coils which you will see being used a lot by locals. But be careful with them as keeping the mosquito coil lit spreads toxic smoke which can be harmful to the body. If you want to use coils, light one and stay away from the room for some time. Avoid inhaling the smoke and make sure to open the doors and windows after some time to let the poisonous smoke go out. These coils are handy if you are staying in rural areas and if you are staying at hotels then most likely you will not have use them.

Eco-friendly smoke

In many rural areas especially in eastern India, you may find a 'Dhunuchi' being lit at dusk. Dried coconut fiber strips are placed inside an earthen container with a handle and the strips are lit. The smoke from the dried coconut strips is supposed to be effective in keeping away mosquitoes. Don't try this at hotels but do feel free to try them if you happen to be staying in rural areas of India.

Avoid spraying strong perfumes

Intense perfumes are known to attract mosquitoes so tone down on your perfumes or lotions in order to avoid becoming an easy target.

Insect swatters and vaporizers

These battery-operated contraptions are handheld devices that can be used to kill bugs. Their length makes it easy to swat mosquitoes even at a distance. Electric vaporizers are also known to be effective and are available in many local stores. Just go and ask your nearest local store while you are in India.

Avoid stagnant water

During the monsoon in India, puddles on the road accumulate that then becomes a breeding ground for mosquitoes. Although you cannot do much about the puddles on the road, you can take some precautions where you are staying. One way to end the menace right at the root is to avoid having stagnant water around the place you are staying. Make sure the bathtubs, buckets, corners etc. do not contain stagnant water. If you have flowerpots in your room or the balcony then make sure you empty them regularly to avoid water accumulation. Also do not have cans and tins lying about as they easily collect water and can become a magnet for mosquitoes. Basically avoid and eliminate all water that is stagnant.

Stay away from dense leafy areas

Dark dense leafy areas often have a concentration of mosquitoes. It might be a good idea to avoid these places particularly after dusk. Try not to stay too long in dark areas generally if you are unprepared to ward off mosquito attacks.

Dress to avoid mosquitoes

It is also said that mosquitoes are attracted to dark colored clothing. Earth colors like beige, brown or green that are close to colors seen in nature are okay. It is a good idea to stick to light colors when you dress. Also make sure you wear full sleeved clothing so that you can cover your arms and legs hence avoiding mosquitoes.

Nylon screen/wire mesh

If you are planning to stay in India for longer duration then it might be a good idea to Install wire mesh on doors and windows of the house which is known to be effective in keeping away mosquitoes. Many Indian homes also have nylon insect screens that can be attached easily to the windows. Make sure you close the windows after sunset as this is this time when the mosquitoes become active. This technique may not be practical if you are staying in India for short periods but if you are planning to stay in India for longer periods then you might consider trying this out.

Remember mosquitoes are a health hazard in India and you must come prepared.

15. Foods to avoid

India is known for its interesting varieties of food but if you are new to the country and its flavors then it is best to avoid certain foods. The reasons for this are many. The ever-present heat causes bacteria to proliferate. In addition, hygienic practices and standards are not always enforced either in cooking or serving except in home settings so the combination of active bacteria and poor hygienic practices can end up causing serious stomach upsets.

Another reason to avoid certain foods is that many people who are visiting the country for the first time fall ill due to the general spiciness of Indian food. If your stomach is not used to Indian spices or chilies then it is best to avoid spicy dishes.

When it comes to Indian food, you often hear stories that sound contrary and confusing. For example, a person may complain that a particular food made them ill, while another person may report being perfectly fine even after eating that item. The simple reason is that some people are able to digest certain foods while some aren't.

So if you are coming to India for the first time then it might be a good idea to avoid some kinds of food and choose food prepared with fresh ingredients under hygienic conditions. But to be honest, you just can't tell if the food you are ordering is alright to eat or not.

Generally speaking, here are some common foods that most visitors to India should avoid if they can.

Not all milk sold in India is properly pasteurized. In fact, most of the milk you will get will come directly from sellers who milk their cows and sell the milk to businesses. However, milk sold by government sources will be pasteurized. The climate in India is such that it encourages growth of bacteria. Therefore, unless milk is heated and boiled thoroughly, you just don't know if the milk is safe or not. Milk that is used in roadside tea or 'chai' is usually safe as boiling kills the bacteria. Avoid any chilled milk or milk that is lukewarm. If in doubt, just speak to the chef or confirm with the waiter if the milk has been pasteurized or boiled properly.

Although ice-cream is relatively safe but you need to be a little careful. Ice-creams in India are often kept in cold storage for long periods encouraging bacterial formation. Look out for ice formation in the ice-cream. This will tell you that the ice-cream has been thawed several times and then been re-cooled.

Similarly, avoid ice cubes, be it in alcoholic drinks, cold beverages or fruit juices. In addition, avoid dips like pudina/coconut chutneys or sauces served with some Indian snacks.

Lassi is a drink made of plain yoghurt diluted with water while raita is a yoghurt dip mixed with raw vegetables is commonly eaten in India. If you do have lassi, make sure the water is of good quality. It may not be a good idea to eat raita as the yogurt may not be fresh. Besides, raita has raw vegetables like cucumbers and onions and you may not know if those vegetables have been properly washed or not.

Avoid all raw vegetables and leaves in your dishes. If you are not too sure about the water used to wash the vegetables or whether they have been washed thoroughly you can skip the salads. Similarly, avoid uncooked and cut fruits. If you can peel the fruit yourself then it should be fine.

As soon as food starts cooling, it becomes a thriving ground for bacteria. So always insist on hot meals and avoid cold salads, lukewarm food or any food that you suspect has been reheated and served.

Skip the food served at weddings and big functions with buffet menus or dishes cooked for large numbers of people. Food for these large gatherings is often made several hours in advance and might contain substandard or stale ingredients that are masked cleverly with spices and sauces.

Many people avoid meat and fish-based dishes during their stay in India. The trouble with fish and meat is the source and also you don't know how long they have been kept in storage.

Another item many people avoid is street food because vendors do not usually follow cleanliness standards. Some street foods to avoid include paani puri, chaat sprinkled with chutney and curd or roadside sambhar.

The golden rule is:

Stick to foods that are freshly prepared for you and avoid those where you do not trust the conditions of the kitchen. A crowded restaurant is indicative of large turnover of ingredients hence they might be safer then where there are no or less people. Ask for popular restaurants or outlets in the area at the hotel.

But do remember these are not hard and fast rules, you just have to make a judgment call there and then and have to decided if you are okay with the food or not. Most high end hotels and restaurants will serve food that have been properly prepared so it will all depend where you are staying and where you decide to eat. If in doubt just ask the waiter or whoever seems to be in charge.

16. Is meat and fish safe in India?

Indian cuisine is famous across the world for its colors, flavors and amazing varieties of tastes. Yet you hear many stories of how visitors to the country tried lots of delicious dishes and ended up with serious stomach ailments - some even leading to hospital visits. Meat and fish are considered the major culprits for the stomach upsets causing many foreigner tourists to suffer. This is entirely due to the fact that they are not taking adequate dietary precautions in India.

I suggest that one of the first things visitors do when they arrive is that they temporarily come vegetarian. Vegetarian cuisine in India is rich and well-developed with each province specializing in uniquely flavored vegetarian dishes. So much so that not even meat-lovers will miss meat or fish on their Indian vacation. In fact, when I am in certain parts of India, I also become vegetarian. It seems a lot safer to eat vegetarians dishes compared to meat dishes.

The subcontinent is a very hot place and chances of food getting bad are very high. Basically food rots quickly in the hot climate. Meat and fish already contain disease-causing bacteria like salmonella and coliform bacteria and in India it's even easier for these bacteria to thrive and multiply in fish, poultry and meat. Locals don't suffer too much from eating the meat/fish as they have developed a resistance to them over the years.

The trouble is not with the ingredients or how it's prepared or served; the trouble is with the storage of the raw materials. Restaurants are not always too particular about how they handle the raw ingredients or about the cleaning mechanisms. If meat or fish are not cleaned properly or if they are served in unclean utensils, it's natural to have stomach infections.

Many places in the country lack adequate facilities for cold storage so meat and fish cannot be preserved well. Vegetables are usually easier to keep at least for a little more time than meat or fish.

It is best to eat fish or meat that's not been kept in the fridge for too long. 1-2 days is okay but after that, it can be a tad too risky as meat or fish get spoiled easily. Besides, there are frequent power cuts so even if the restaurant has a deep fridge, the meat/fish can still go bad. It should be quite easy to smell fish/meat that has gone bad. But what many restaurants do is that they disguise the spoilt fish or meat with a variety of spices and sauces. So, when you eat that fiery looking chicken curry or that deliciously creamy prawn curry, you may be risking a serious infection.

If you do happen to go to the fish or meat market, you will see that they are sold openly. You will see flies resting on the raw meat and fish. It's a not a lovely site. In addition, if raw meat or fish are kept in the open for too long, they become easy targets for the bacteria present in the air.

Consider all these reasons and it may seem like a good idea to skip meat/fish in India altogether. But the truth it is that not all meat/fish in India are always unsafe. In coastal areas where seafood or fish is plentiful and locally available and prepared right in front of you, I am sure you can enjoy them without any issues. Goa is one place where you should be able to get plenty of fresh fish. If in doubt, you can always ask where the fish and poultry are coming from.

Here are a few addition tips

Avoid meat/fish at large gatherings. Usually, this is where cold-storage fish or meat may be used and the danger levels with regard to infection can be quite high. Many locals too get food poisoning after eating at weddings or other large social gatherings.

You can have meat/seafood or fish when you know they are absolutely fresh. Usually, if you are invited to an Indian friend's house for a special meal, you can more or less be sure that the ingredients used are fresh. Indians are serious about welcoming guests so they will get the best and freshest ingredients. Non-vegetarian restaurants that are popular with locals are usually safe. In any circumstances if you are unsure just ask about the freshness of the meat/fish particularly if you are in a restaurant.

Since pork is not processed in safe conditions in most parts of India, avoid eating pork.

17. Guide to Indian street food

Crunchy, salty, tangy, sweet, colorful and varied - street foods sold on the lanes and by-lanes of India symbolize the heterogeneous spirit of the country. You will find these tasty dishes are eaten by locals as swiftly as the vendor seated at the cart or on the footpath can make them. Whether it is sticky sweet jalebis in Agra, the crunchy potato-based snacks in Jaipur, the 'ragda patties' in Mumbai, spicy egg rolls wrapped with thin paper in Kolkata, or flavorful kebabs in Old Delhi - watching vendors make their special dishes is a treat in itself - you feel like you are watching a conjurer performing tricks.

Let's come to the real question. Should you eat them or not? The answer is yes and no.

Many people choose to refrain from eating street food during their Indian sojourn but if you are the adventurous type then you may want to try them. Curiously enough, street food can actually be safer than food prepared in restaurants or big buffet spreads at five star hotels. The reason is that you don't really know when the food was prepared. Perhaps it was prepared the previous night or it's the left over's from the previous buffet. Unless it is an open kitchen style arrangement or you can peek into the kitchen of the restaurant, you don't really know the ins and outs of those dishes brought to your table. Whereas with street food - what you see is what you get right before your eyes.

Here's a brief guide to enjoy street food safely in India

Many street food items are cooked in oil. If you want to try fried fritters such as vegetables dipped in a batter and deep fried (known as pakora), insist on the item being prepared in front of you. Avoid those fried items that either look stale or are cold or those that have been prepared in advance and are on display. The oil used to fry the street food dishes is often not very good but if you stick to those vendors who seem to be popular with the locals then the risk is limited. The rest is left to chance and the strength of your immune system as is the case most of the time with Indian street food.

With street food, you do not know how clean the utensils are. A good idea may be to carry your own container and ask the vendor to fill it with the item. You can also keep a spoon handy with you. Just tuck it into your side bag if you are planning to explore the streets in any Indian city. Most cities and towns are known for their famous street foods so you can try them while not risking contamination at least from utensils.

Many street food vendors are not too keen about cleaning the dishes even though they may have fabulously artful ways of preparing and presenting the food item they are selling. The water used to clean the utensils is usually best not spoken about and in fact many diseases pass through contaminated water in India. To avoid this, it is a good idea to use your own water to wash the utensil if you are eating off the plates provided by the vendor. You could ask for the plate and give it a rinse with your own bottled water.

It is a good idea also to skip any dish that is cold, has too much water or uses sauces you aren't sure about. For example, if you are having Bhel Puri, you can ask the vendor to skip the green sauce.

You will see temptingly arranged plates of cut fruits on carts on the streets. You never know when these fruits were cut so avoid them. Instead, buy whole fruits, peel and wash and then eat. You will also find many vendors who cut the fruits/vegetables (like cucumbers, raw mangos etc) and add some spicy powder for taste and sell them. These can be fine safety wise if you can handle the spiciness. But make sure that fruits have been cut in front of your eyes.

Avoid ice lollies from the roadside. Sometimes the water and coloring ingredients used in them may not be safe for consumption.

Fruit juices such as sugarcane juice or orange juice are more or less safe but do make sure that they have been squeezed in front of you. Just bring your own glass if you can.

One of the most famous Indian street food is none other than the famous 'gol guppa', also known as 'paani puri' or 'phuchka' eaten with spicy-water. But if you want to give this dish a try then you might ask the vendor to skip the water. Other thing you can do is ask the vendor to make you the spicy-water with bottled mineral water which is going to be a lot safer for you.

You can avoid many of these waterborne diseases if you have your jabs particularly hepatitis A and the cholera vaccinations before you come to India.

I am not trying to scare you or anything; you just need to be careful with street food.

18. Travelling in India during the monsoons

Monsoons are a very welcome change on the subcontinent and travelling in this season has many perks. Many people would advise you against touring India during the monsoon months given the mud and slime, and the difficulties of navigating the treacherous and ill-maintained Indian roads. But if you have no troubles with some dirt, and do not mind the rain or traffic slowdowns then there is much to enjoy during the monsoons of India.

The green scenery

As the scorching heat gives way to heavy monsoon downpours, much of the Indian landscape gets transformed. The verdant beauty of the hills in places like Khandala, Mahabaleshwar and Ooty is breathtaking. In Kerala, the lagoons with the green coconut trees reflected in them look resplendent after every shower of rain.

Opportunities to enjoy seasonal festivals

The monsoons have been traditionally regarded as a festive season in India because it nurtures the crops in the fields. You can travel to various parts of India and enjoy the songs, dances and colorful celebrations associated with monsoon festivals some of which include Onam the harvest festival of Kerala, the Ratha Yatra festival in many parts of Eastern India, and unique festivals of Northeastern India such as the Nongkrem Dance and the Reh Festival.

The discounted prices

If you are looking to enjoy India away from the touristy crowds then the monsoons can be a great time to travel. Most hotels and airlines offer discounted prices during this time, so you can make fabulous savings on your tours. In addition, at most places you go there won't be too much of a holidaying crowd, so you can bask in the rain-washed atmosphere and enjoy the sights in peace.

Colors, dance, song, beautiful and vibrant costumes and of course, getting wet are all part of enjoying monsoon magic in India.

Ensure that you take proper precautions to make the most of your trip. Here are some monsoon tips.

Eat safely

The monsoons are a happy time for germs thanks to the rampant prevalence of poor hygiene conditions. Make sure you eat and drink safely. Avoid tap water, street food, cut fruits and salads. It is more or less safe to drink tea or coffee since boiling the water kills most germs. Buy bottled water, carry dry snacks and fruits in airtight containers, during your travels in the monsoons. Stock up on local items that can be easily preserved such as puffed rice, biscuits, cereals etc for emergencies just in case you are stranded on the road due to water logging or some other reason during the heavy rains.

Be prepared

Wear clothes that drip and dry with long sleeves to protect against bugs and carry umbrellas or raincoats with you. Carry a torch as stormy weather can suddenly cause electricity failures. Have anti-mosquito repellents in your first aid kit and ask your doctor about the vaccinations you may need to be protected against common water-borne diseases before you come to India. Mosquito nets, bug swatters and locally available creams like Odomos are some ways you can keep away mosquitoes.

Keep updated on road conditions

The monsoons are a time when everything becomes quite unpredictable. Keep enough buffer time on your hands and maintain flexibility in your planning. Uprooted trees blocked roads, snapped electricity lines, storms, landslides and more are part and parcel of monsoons in India. The mountains come alive after the rains and the waterfalls are a grand sight but also be aware of the risks of slippery road surfaces and flash floods, before you set out especially if you are trekking. Be careful if your plans involve long road trips.

Be realistic

In many parts of India, national parks and sanctuaries remain closed throughout the monsoon months. If you plan to enjoy animal watching and bird sightings during this period, you may have to go away disappointed. Also keep interacting with locals to learn about the ground conditions wherever you are. You will get a fair idea of which roads to avoid, which river is risky to cross and so on.

Come prepared during the monsoons. A bit of humor and ability to bear snags and changes in your travel plans can go a long way but other than that your monsoon tours in India can be truly memorable.

Check weather reports

Always keep an eye on the weather report. Here are some sites that can you use.

http://www.weather-forecast.com/countries/India

http://www.weatherforecastmap.com/india

http://www.bbc.co.uk/weather/1269750

http://weather.edition.cnn.com/weather/intl/forecast.jsp

19. Types of transport in India

India is a country of many layers which is reflected in the country's many varieties of transport. Some transportation modes go back centuries while some are much more recent. On your Indian sojourns, depending on whether you are travelling by water or by land, over short distances or long, you will end up using many of the transport systems, both public and private.

Let's take a look at some of the types of transport available in the country.

Air Transport - Flights

For swift travel between far-flung places in India, flights are commonly used these days by middle class Indians. Indian Airlines is the official government owned air carrier while Air India is partly government owned and there are numerous private carriers like Jet Airways, SpiceJet, Jet Airways,

Indigo Airlines, GoAir etc. You should be able to buy air tickets at airports or on their websites - subject to availability.

Road Transport

With about 300,000 kilometers of the land surface connected by roads, the network of Indian roads is undoubtedly one of the worlds largest. There are many types of road from National Highways and State Highways which are usually in a decent motorable condition to city roads, district roads and un-tarred village roads - you will see roads in every condition. Some states and certain rural areas of India will have very poor conditions of their roads. In fact, some places don't even have roads. Nonetheless, tourist sites are well connected and have decent roads.

Trains

As the largest employer in the country, the Indian Railways has a unique position in facilitating everything from sightseeing tours to business trips at economical rates. There are local trains for intra-state travel and long-distance trains like Shatabdi and Duronto Express connecting different states. Long-distance trains have classified travel system with varying price brackets like AC 1st class, 2nd class sleeper class, non-AC and general non-reserved compartment. The Indian Railways are government owned and often the long distance trains have pantry car arrangements. You also find many independent vendors selling snacks on local trains, adding to the colors, sights and cacophony of Indian train journeys.

Buses

Many places in India are connected by trains but for places still beyond the reach of railways, the bus is a popular mode of transport. Within cities, buses are quite common and you will also find buses connecting a city or town with its suburbs. Long-distance buses connect different states and a lot of people travel on overnight buses. State run bus services and private bus services are both common. Usually these are non-AC and crowded. Though privately owned and more expensive the Volvo Bus Services are also becoming popular.

Autos, taxis, cycle rickshaws, cars, motorcycles and the rest

Taxis are common in the metros and big cities. Individual states usually have their standard guidelines for the make and color of the taxi. Taxis are pricier than other kinds of road transport but it lets you travel in relative comfort and privacy - unless you are riding a shared taxi where the taxi works like a shuttle service.

The autos-rickshaws or the three wheelers are useful for short distance travel in cities or towns. Their smaller size lets them conveniently weave through the crowded roads in conditions in which bigger vehicles cannot pass through. The yellow and black autos run on diesel while the green and yellow ones are CNG rules-compliant autos.

Cycle rickshaws also sometimes called 'rickshaw' by locals are common in smaller towns or suburbs of big cities. The driver rides a bicycle while two passengers can sit on a mounted area at the back. A variant of this in small towns is called the van-rickshaw. The driver cycles while the passengers sit on a contraption made of planks at the back dangling their legs. There are no handles or railings so passengers may arrange themselves on all the three sides along the planks.

Horse-driven carriages usually known as 'tonga' are sometimes seen in Agra, Kolkata, Murshidabad and some other places in India. These are the older modes of transport and often carry nostalgic value. In remote areas, people may hitch rides on trucks to go long distances.

Many Indians drive their cars or use car rental services. You also use car rental services for sightseeing purpose. Heavy cars like Toyota, Innova or Bolero are suitable for mountain roads.

Motorbikes can be rode on tough Indian road conditions quite easily and are often considered a classic way to travel and enjoy the local atmosphere. Royal Enfield and local makers like Bajaj, TVS, Hero Honda etc. are common on Indian roads.

Water Transport

Steamers, launch-boats and regular boats with oars are some common water transport modes. There may be regional variations in boats. Some may be even made of eco-friendly local material. In mangrove areas like the Sunderbans, steamers are common. Often in these places, people cross rivers by via big steamers and you find cycles and motorcycles also being carried to the other side. It can be quite a spectacle!

20. How to book train tickets in India?

The Indian Railway, the largest in the world, is one means of transport that connects the entire country. Going to places by train may not be as quick as flying but it is much cheaper and lets you experience the medley of colorful layers, cultures and languages that make up this country. So popular are the railways here that people from all sections of society travel by it. In fact, it is so popular that seats fill up very fast which means that as a traveler, you will have to book tickets well in advance. Typically, when people decide on a place to travel, the first thing they do is to book the train tickets. If you are going to a popular tourist site, it is a good idea to book at least months in advance.

In the earlier times, one would have to go to the station and book tickets at the booking counter that used to open in the morning and closed in the evening. Now, one can do that as well in addition to book e-tickets online making it a lot easier for those using the internet. Usually, you need to get a print-out and display a valid photo identification proof (passport) while producing the print-out for verification.

The Indian Railways has its own website where people can book tickets, but there is a hitch. Sometimes due to a lot of people trying to use the site at the same time and due to the bulky technical infrastructure, the website loads very slowly. So it can be a test of your patience to directly book at the Indian Railways booking site – www.irctc.co.in. An alternative is to book via private travel arrangement sites like MakeMyTrip, ClearTrip, Yatra etc. which have online booking facilities for different elements of travel like hotels, trains, flights etc. All these sites fetch data from the Indian Railways site and are quite reliable hence they have become quite popular with travelers. You need to pay a fee in addition to the price of the ticket on most of these sites.

On long-distance travel from one state to another, most people make reservations. This means that you get your own seat and is confirmed and no one else can occupy it. It is a good idea to book tickets if your travel involves peak tourist seasons, overnight journeys or popular sightseeing places. If you go to any site and look at facilities for booking seats on express or long-distance trains, you find that the Indian reservation system has many categories. The level of comfort and amenities you get on the ride depend on which class you are travelling by and the price you are willing to pay.

There are two common types of compartments - The First Class and the Second Class. The First Class is in which the compartments are air-conditioned and have sleeper/chair car arrangements with on-board meals and towels, bed sheets etc. provided by the railways. Second Class compartments may be AC or non-AC. There is the very crowded General Class compartment in which you can travel without booking and I suggest you avoid this completely even if you're backpacking.

During booking, depending on the extent of the rush, you may or may not be able to confirm your seat. If that is the case, it will be listed as RAC/WL on the site or the person at the counter (if you are booking in person or through an agent) will tell you.

Here are some terminologies

RAC – Reservation Against Cancellation –The seats are all booked, but if anyone cancels his/her reservation, you are next in line for a confirmed seat.

WL - Waiting List - If the RAC status tickets are dealt with and seats confirmed and more seats are left over, only then WL status seats get confirmed. This can be dicey if you are travelling in peak tourist season.

<u>Tatkal arrangements</u> for emergency bookings are available for a higher fee. The Tatkal booking facility opens three days before the journey date.

Most Indian trains these days have some seats reserved especially for foreign tourists in both first and second class compartments. You can also get hold of an IndRail Pass (available in a few countries via agents) which is convenient for transits or short-duration travel. For reservations using these facilities, you need to make the payment in advance in dollars.

You can also book some tickets at the airport. As soon are you are stepping out of the airport after baggage collection, you will see the Indian Railway counter or other travel agents where you can book train tickets with them.

Check the site http://www.indianrail.gov.in/international_Tourist.html for more information. In addition, International Tourist Bureaus established in several Indian cities provide information on booking train tickets and other travel matters for foreign tourists.

21. How to hire a taxi and auto-rickshaw?

Taxis and auto-rickshaws are common ways to travel short to moderate distances. If you are looking to travel to different sightseeing destinations, you can either hire a taxi or an auto-rickshaw to get there quickly and with relative ease. Sometimes people hire the taxi or the auto-rickshaw for the entire day as a convenient arrangement with the driver.

Responding to the demands of tourists, many agencies have come up with taxi rental services that have become quite a popular option. There are many reasons why these taxi rental agencies are becoming popular by both locals and tourists. Firstly, you do not need to go into the hassles of calling a taxi off the street and get into bargains with the driver. You just have to make a call or book the services online to rent a taxi. Neither do you face the risks of being taken for a ride by being led to various places around the city. This often happens if the driver realizes that you do not know your way around. Then he can take a longer route and charge you excessively. Some taxi drivers also tamper with their meters to reflect a higher fare than normal. When you hire a taxi, you cut out all these complications. The rates are pre-decided, you tell the driver for how long you want to use the vehicle, and the driver remains accountable for inept service if any as long as you can get back to the agency with your feedback.

Airports, railway stations and other major destinations in the city are where you often find prepaid taxi services. With the prepaid taxi services, you pay at the counter and then you are given the receipt, you find the taxi at the taxi stand and give the receipt to the driver when you get to the destination.

What are the things to keep in mind when you hire taxis? How do you make the most of whichever rental service you choose?

Take a look at this quick guide to hire a taxi

When you avail rental services by major agencies like Meru Cabs, Mega Cabs or Easy Cabs, keep some time in hand. With some agencies, you need to book in advance before the rental service sends a taxi. To get a taxi at the time you require, you may even need to make a booking at least 24 hours in advance. Depending on the requirements and duration of the trip, some agencies may even be able to send their taxi in 15-30 minutes. So, whether it is a holiday trip you're taking or need to catch a flight, do make sure to get the booking done at the right time.

Find out what modes of payment the taxi rental service recognizes. There are some agencies that accept payment both by cash and credit/debit cards easing the business of hiring a taxi for international tourists. So, if you still have not converted your money to Indian Rupees or have just arrived in the country, a debit/credit card payment saves you the hassle.

Most large rental agencies have fleets with AC and non-AC vehicles. If you are travelling in very hot weather, you may need an air-conditioned taxi to beat the heat but have to pay a little extra. On the contrary, if the weather is cool and pleasant, you may not need an air conditioned cab.

Many rental agencies have a fleet of cars of different capacities to serve as taxis. Let the agency know the size of your travelling group and pick a suitable vehicle. Often, if you have a lot of luggage, you need a big sedan/saloon or an SUV like the Innova or the Bolero. Find out if there are extra charges for carrying luggage.

While taxis are great for sustained sightseeing or comfortable transits between different points, you can also have auto-rickshaws for short trips. If you are a small group of travelers, you can hire an entire auto for yourself, but autos are mostly comfortable for 25-30 km long trips and not more. Whatever the vehicle you hire; taxi or auto-rickshaw just agree on the rate beforehand to prevent being fleeced. Ask for rate charts if necessary and if you are travelling at night or want to make stops on your ride to get down and see tourist landmarks, find out about the extra charges. Make sure you discuss beforehand how long you intend to stop at a certain location and decide the fare accordingly.

22. Guide to prepaid taxis

If you are a visitor in India, taxis work well to take you not only from the airport to the hotel, but also to get around in the city or town you are visiting. Indian taxis are supposed to run on meters but sometimes the driver may persist in overcharging or try to dupe you in some other way. It may get worse if you are unfamiliar with the roads when the driver quite literally can take you for a ride. This is why prepaid taxis have come popular not only amongst tourists but also locals. These taxis make the journeys hassle-free for all sorts of people. Prepaid taxis give you a stress-free way to travel by being accountable at almost every step.

Here's guide to prepaid taxis in India

Prepaid taxi booths

In prepaid taxis, you stand in line with others, waiting for your turn at a prepaid taxi booth. It may take a little more time than casually catching a taxi but the safety and security is often worth it. At these booths, which you find at airports, railway stations and central locations in many big Indian cities, you need to tell them about your destination, make the payment and proceed to the taxi stand. The prepaid taxis at the Delhi International airport are operated by the Delhi Transport so chances of incidences are slim.

Preset fare

When you choose a prepaid taxi option, the amount is decided beforehand. This is not something a taxi driver can just tell you but it is determined by the fare chart, approved by the local government. At most prepaid taxi counters, you can see a rate chart clearly displayed. This means no danger of being fleeced by unscrupulous drivers. Plus, you know that the amount being charged is legitimate and government approved.

Taxi voucher

You get a voucher at the prepaid taxi booth and you will need to retain it till the end-point of your journey. The voucher is a record of the details of the journey from your point of destination to where you are going along with other necessary details. Once you get off, hand over your voucher to the driver. Since this voucher contains important information like the taxi number, distance covered, etc. it also acts as a documentary proof in case anything goes wrong during the trip.

All the Indian metros and big cities like Mumbai, Delhi, Kolkata, Bengaluru and Hyderabad have public prepaid taxi services. Many tourist centers also have introduced these services to make trips easy and tension-free for travelers and more are soon to follow. These prepaid taxis are authorized vehicles so there is no danger of running foul with the local rules and the fare itself.

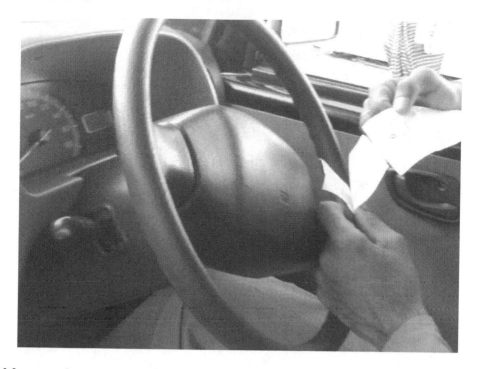

Many private agencies like Meru, Easy Cabs and Cool Cab also run prepaid taxi services which are popular, safe and convenient. Depending on which agency you choose, you can pre-book online or call them up on their toll-free numbers to make your booking. Just find their numbers or use their booking form online. You can also choose air-conditioned taxis in the summer to beat the heat. Prepaid private taxi services are quite common outside international airports of Mumbai and Bengaluru. Some agencies offer a few extras for example; you can use your credit card if you do not have the local currency and pay the driver at the end of the journey.

The transparent and systematic approach of prepaid taxis has become so popular that locals too prefer them over regular ones. Among the many advantages of prepaid taxis, one of them is that you know exactly the amount you have to pay. Since this is a prepaid amount, you do not have to run into endless bargaining matches with the driver. Make the payment, get into the assigned taxi and ride in safety.

Very recently at Howrah station in Kolkata, I realized the value of prepaid taxis all over again. I was back with friends from a trip and they were to go from Howrah to Santoshpur. At the prepaid taxi counter, the big blue new rate chart conveniently displayed the rate – Rs 250. My friends still wanted to scout around to get an estimate of what regular, that is, non-prepaid taxis would charge. The drivers we approached all had different reactions. One flatly said he did not know the place, another said it was too far, a third grinned and demanded Rs 400! Ultimately, we took a prepaid taxi and leaned back in our seats. It was time to enjoy the journey.

23. Safety on Indian trains

Indian trains offer a ride of a truly unique kind, filled with the cultural madness and complexity that characterizes India. In order to experience some of the country you must get on the great Indian train. While Indian trains offer a varied and adventurous experience, it pays to be safe and secure.

Here are some guidelines to staying safe and enjoying the Indian train ride.

Securing the main luggage

If you are travelling long distances then you most probably will have several pieces of luggage. Train rides can be as short as six hours to a day and a half or more. Your luggage needs complete protection all times when you are on the train - from the moment you get on to the moment you get off. What most passengers do is push heavy or large luggage below the seat. Many people also put some of their main luggage on the topmost bunk if it is empty. Wherever you place your luggage, remember to lock it. Some trolley bags and other luggage items come with their own lock and key or have combination lock systems – use it. At stations, you also get chains, which is great to secure your main luggage in place. This serves a dual purpose. It keeps your luggage safe and secured even if the train lurches and it prevents the luggage from being stolen. Invest in a strong chain that cannot be cut with a pair of pliers. Secure all the pouches of your main luggage as well as you can before you get on the train.

Use a hand bag

Trains do not have a lot of space which means it is not a good idea to open your main luggage during the ride. Instead, have a hand bag in which you can carry the essentials you need on the train. A few everyday items like cosmetics, toothbrush, soap, comb, mirror, and other items you need can be placed in the hand bag and taken out when required. If you are travelling on an overnight train or want to sleep during some part of the ride, you can do what many locals do which is nod-off for a while but do make sure your luggage is safe and secure. One way to do this is to use the important piece of luggage as a pillow or keep it snug on one side while you sleep.

Be careful with money

It is a good idea to carry your money in a hand bag which stays with you all the time. Many people keep some part of the money deep inside the luggage where it cannot be reached, for example an inner pocket, a secret pouch or the lining inside a bag. Either way it is a good idea to split up the money you are carrying instead of having it all collected in one place.

Be careful about co-passengers

Maintain your distance with co-passengers and do not get over-friendly. Do not accept food from any stranger during the ride as the food may contain sedatives or drugs that are designed to make you fall asleep. While you are asleep, you are robbed of your belongings - sadly something like this does happen. We as Indians get to read about such incidences in the newspapers all the time. Buy your own food or carry your own instead, to remain safe. The food provided by the railways is safe to eat.

Using the toilet

Whatever the kind of toilet you go to, Western style or squat style on an Indian train, you find that the space is very cramped. It is risky to use the toilet while the train is at full-speed because a lurch or bend may throw you off-balance. Try to use the toilet just before the train picks up speed. For example a good idea to use the toilets is just after a train has left a station. When you are in the toilet, hold on to the hand-bar to keep your balance.

Hand hooks on unreserved compartments

If you are on a short distance journey then you may be tempted to risk an unreserved ride. Unreserved compartments are those where anyone can sit anywhere they like and you may even have to remain standing up for the whole duration of your journey. Just in case the compartments are crowded and you have to stand up then hold on to the hand hooks to help you stand up. If you don't find a seat and have to remain standing then grip the hand hook usually made of leather dangling from the ceiling well to avoid falling.

24. Dealing with beggars

With a teeming population in almost every state, India can be a shock for people on the first encounter. It is difficult to forget the strangeness of this country even on repeated visits. What adds to the strangeness is the presence of people begging everywhere be it at metro stations, railway stations, near tourist spots, temples, mosques and even at traffic lights. The question is - how do you deal with beggars? Is there any right way to treat people who are begging? The answer is that there's no clear straight-cut answer and like many things in India, it is a good idea to keep your mind open, and deal with every situation on a case-by-case basis.

In India, you will hear many horror stories about begging. Many beggars are roped into the profession after their limbs are chopped off, mothers or families push their children onto the street, and evil people run organized begging rackets where beggars are hauled up for not producing enough money at the end of the day.

Foreign tourists are soft targets by beggars as it is automatically assumed that they are always loaded with cash. Why are foreign tourists targeted? There are several reasons for this. Well, foreign Western tourists do not know what to do when they encounter beggars. The beggars know this very well. They often get frightened when they see beggars. Beggars in India are not like the ones you see on the London tube station entrances or streets of New York who ask for spare change. The beggars in India do look extremely poor and many of the times they carry babies to trigger human emotions of their targets. Sometimes, many beggars will have limbs that are twisted or even cut off. There will be child beggars. When foreign tourists see these things, they feel pity and give in and end up handing out large sums of money to these beggars. Even we Indians feel the same way.

Let's face, it is a sad sight and not something people want to see especially if you are on a holiday. But begging in India is a sad reality. But mind you, in the last several decades, lots of people have been uplifted out of poverty and many beggars on the streets are fake beggars out there to make a quick buck. But at the same time, there are real beggars that do need our kind consideration.

If you are a visitor in the country, you will find locals using some of these ways to deal with beggars.

- Do not look at the beggar and pretend they don't exist.

- Completely ignore the hand asking for change.

- Say go away to the beggar (Agay badho).

- Wave their hand asking the beggar to go away.

- Make eye contact and say a firm NO (Nahi in Hindi).

- Give some loose change to the beggar and move on.

- Hand the person some food (chocolate bar for instance) or candies. If they are hungry, they will accept the food and move away.

Many places in India always have a cluster of beggars, such as the entrance of temples where many people are lined up, sitting or standing and waiting for generous devotees to hand some money. While many Indians get by just giving some money, foreigners may get circled in by large groups of beggars. You may find requests for more, demands and entreaties or even abuses by beggars for ignoring them. Say 'No' (Nahi) emphatically and walk away if you are uncomfortable being touched. You can also say that you won't give any money if people insist on touching you.

Opinions are divided on begging. Some people give only to beggars who genuinely can't earn a living any other way like very old people. Some people say giving encourages laziness. Or the beggars will use the money to buy cheap drugs like sniffing glue or ganja and so on. Some argue that if you stop giving then begging will die out! Others say, not giving does little to end the surging population of new beggars, as sometimes people lose their limited social security net and end up on the street. India has no social security net for large sections of the population or official facilities for rehabilitating beggars. In India, people do not get any benefits, social security or tax credits of any kind and many people do end up on the streets.

Some non-governmental organizations do serious long-term work, such as taking children off the street and putting them in schools, or providing warm clothing in winter, or taking care of their food requirements. Many people choose to donate to Non Government Organizations (NGOs) where they know the money will be put to good use instead of trying to help beggars on an individual basis. Undoubtedly, without collective effort and an understanding of how and why people get into begging, both on the part of the government, NGOs and individuals, begging cannot gradually and humanely be phased out in India.

I still remember the first time a beggar touched me. The auto was at a signal in Patna and I found a hand touching my knee. A light brush, but I twitched, extremely unnerved and looked to see a small girl near the auto. I didn't know what to do and was visibly shaken. I'd bought some clothes in Mumbai, and was rejecting my older clothes. The next time the auto was at the signal, the small girl was near the auto again. This time, I gave her a reject dress in decent wearable condition. The third time, the auto moved ahead on an empty road, but when I looked back, I found the small girl delightedly wearing my dress. Till date, I find myself dealing with beggars on a situational basis, and there are still emotional conflicts inside. The challenge is to face the situation and still remain humane.

25. How to deal with touts?

Travelling in India can offer a lot of surprises and rich experiences but it pays to be careful and keep your eyes open wherever you travel especially against touts. You cannot avoid the presence of these innocent sounding and absolutely unscrupulous people whose aim is to cheat you whatever way they can. Taking advantage of India's phenomenal tourism industry, unscrupulous middle-men or touts have become a common sight at railway stations, airports, outside transport hubs of tourist centers, near hotels and temples. Often, people fall into the clutches of touts and have to part with their hard-earned money or end up with other material losses. There are many ways to deal with touts and keep yourself protected in India.

Once, I was at Howrah station with a few friends and our destination was a place in Kolkata. We were discussing which way to go, how long it would take to get there, and so on. Soon we found several friendly looking taxi drivers looming over us. One of them looked friendly and asked in detail about where we were going. A few questions and answers later, feeling a bit assured, my friends asked him his rate. 'Rupees 400', he grinned back. 'Not one rupee less'.

[121]

That's when it hit me that we were talking to a tout. Then I urged my friends to do what seemed right in the circumstance which was to say no and move on.

Take a look at some of the ways to tackle the tout menace while you are in India.

Say a firm No – NAHI....

It can seem scary to be pressed in by over-eager people when you arrive at your destination. Some may promise a cheap way to reach your hotel, some may suggest they have a reliable car to take you there, or make some other offer. Touts often are found operating hand in hand, at the same place, so as soon as one comes up to you, you may often find others following suit. Often the best way to stop the issue from getting out of hand is to say a firm 'No' right at the beginning. As soon as my friends and I realized we were being targeted by a tout for the taxi ride, we said 'No' (Nahi), began ignoring anything he said and walked right ahead.

Stick to your stand

If you stick to your stand, it is often a great way to dissuade prospective touts. If you already have a hotel booked or transport waiting to receive you - tell the tout. Even if you don't, look confident and assured. A little hesitancy on your part means you give room for the tout to sidle in and make fresh offers. So make clear eye contact and say no and then break the eye contact firmly and confidently and brush your way past them.

Use authorized means

Touts are usually illegitimate operators out there to make a quick buck so look for authorized agencies wherever you can. Because of these touts, prepaid taxis have become popular. After running into this tout who was insisting on Rupees 400 for the trip, we decided to head to the prepaid taxi counter where the amount to travel a route is fixed and written on a display board. During non-prepaid taxi rides, if you find yourself getting suspicious, ask for the fare chart. Taxi drivers are compulsorily required to have one inside and show it to their passenger on demand.

Be clear about payments

Sometimes someone may approach you and tell you that they will show you around a certain area and you can pay later. Don't ever except something like this. It may seem a good idea at that time but be clear about payments.

At temples and other such places where you may be a stranger to local customs, find out the prices if you are asked to participate in certain ceremonies. If you feel pressurized by those asking for donations then just step away. Be well-versed in how local currency works and the conversion rates and count the change carefully when you get it back. Do your homework about places to which you are going and stick to well-known agencies wherever possible.

Guides at historical places

You will find 'guides' that will want to show you around. Some are government approved while some are not. If your travel agency or hotel has not fixed a guide for you then you might want to hire one. As soon you step into a historical monument, some guides will follow you and ask if you want one. If they are approved guides then they will wear a badge and will have some sort of identification to prove it. If you do want a guide to show you around then by all means hire one. But again be clear with the prices and fix it.

Many of these guides are not touts and therefore are actually working as guides. However some guides are touts and vice versa. If you do hire a guide and they start coming up with other offers then you know that they could be a tout.

26. How to be safe at the hotel?

Hotels are supposed to be the most secure of all places. It is here that you can go and sleep and then be ready for your next day. Unfortunately there have been a few incidences at Indian hotels which make you think if you should carefully examine the type of hotel you are staying in. Wherever you travel, be it India or elsewhere, it is a good idea to follow some safety guidelines.

Here are some common hotel safety rules

Research the hotel if possible

Many hotels are listed on online forums and review sites where other travelers' review and grade hotels based on their services, accommodation and safety standards. Check them out. You can also ask colleagues in India or acquaintances if you have any about hotel recommends. Also, five-star and four-star hotels usually tend to have higher safety standards than medium-range hotels. So if you can afford to spend a little extra for safety then do so. Even in up market hotels, remain careful and do not divulge too much information about yourself to the hotel staff or get too chatty with the attendants.

If you have special requirements, like a women-'s only corridor or floor, or need accessibility options in the hotel, do your research carefully. Some Indian hotels these days provide cell phones to women guests and have extra security for women. Do your research and clarify your safety concerns before you check in.

Assess the surroundings

Find out a bit about the area where the hotel is situated. If it is a bazaar area, you can ask for a room if possible, away from the road, so that your room is not visible outright to any potential burglar. Some medium-rung hotels have windows in some rooms facing the staff area. If you do not want to be disturbed by the noise of the hotel staff going about their work or risk seeing a face peeping in through the window, you can avoid rooms in such busy areas of the hotel.

Go through the room carefully

Before taking a room, watch out for windows or doors that will not close properly. Check the latches to see if they work. Look in the bathroom and behind the doors. Keep your eyes open for hidden mirrors or other objects that could be used to spy on you.

Know the emergency exits

This is important in case there is a fire outbreak at the hotel. Find out about the hotel's emergency evacuation plans at the start. Ask about fire extinguishers. Know the way from your room to the emergency exit, and stay prepared.

Maintain your privacy

The practice many Indian hotels follow is that the guest leaves the room key with the person at the lobby and claims it on return. While telling the receptionist or person at the lobby your room number, make sure you are not overheard.

You can also insist on keeping the duplicate keys with you all the time.

Remain alert every time you come into and leave your room

Make sure the room is locked before you leave. If it a regular lock then place the key in the lock twice to ensure it is locked. When you come into your room again after a period of absence, look around carefully before entering. Also, make sure no one is in the room by checking thoroughly behind curtains, doors, and the bathroom or under the bed. If you feel unsure about your safety, ask the lobby to have a bellboy accompany you to your room.

Maintain safety in your room

When you are in then seal the door and for extra precaution push a heavy piece of furniture (a side-table, chair etc.) against the door. You don't have to do all the time, just before you go to sleep. Open the door only when you are sure it is a hotel attendant and verify the identity if possible, if the door has a keyhole or spyglass. If you are suspicious, call the lobby and confirm if they have sent an attendant. Before sleeping, double check all the security arrangements, and if the windows face the hotel corridor or the street, lock the windows.

Safety of belongings

Do not keep valuables, the wallet, passport, credit cards or documents with personal information etc. lying about. Lock the zips of all bags before going out. Also, a smart tip many cautious travelers use is to keep their belongings arranged in a specific manner. If anyone has been looking among your belongings, you would know then at once. Many hotels provide safe deposit arrangements for a fee. Paying a little extra for safety is often a good idea.

27. How to be safe in Indian crowds?

One of the biggest shocks for many people coming for the first time to India is the amount of people they see. From shops, to roads, to trains, there just seem to be too many people everywhere. It is a country of more than a billion people, with babies being born all the time, so needless to say, crowd are often one of the main things to deal with when you come to India.

Dealing with the city footpaths

While walking, you may often have to deal with the crowded conditions on the footpaths. In some places, you can choose the less crowded footpath between the ones on the right and left sides of the road. Usually places with few vendors are less crowded, but you cannot completely avoid crowds even if you travel in cars, as you will have to get out and sightsee a bit on foot. Most Indian cities are overcrowded and in urban tours you will just have to get used to this.

Dealing with the traffic

Keep enough time in hand to reckon for traffic jams and the crowded road conditions. If you have taken a taxi or hired a car and if there is more than one road to reach a destination, you can ask the driver to choose the road that's likely to have traffic. For this though, you need to either have a local with you, or have spent enough time in the city to be knowledgeable about which roads are busier than others.

Dealing with the crowds in villages

Indian crowds are often a friendly and curious lot so whether in cities or villages, you as a foreigner may be at the receiving end of much staring. Get used to some of the unabashed staring, especially if you are travelling in a big car on narrow village roads. Many villagers may simply be gawking at the car rather than at you personally. You may also in many places get requests for being photographed. It's up to you to refuse politely or agree to a snapshot clicked by a local.

Dealing with roads

Sometimes you will realize that road rules are not being followed. Basically people do what they want, cross the road how they want and where they want and so on. Many roads may not have zebra crossings, or the traffic may be chaotic. You will see that many of us Indians across the road in groups. Some even gesture for the traffic to stop by showing their hands up. You can fall into one of these groups and cross safely as vehicles usually stop when people are crossing roads en masse.

Dealing with the noise

Noise is one of the top features of Indian roads. Not only do you have to deal with incessant honking from vehicles but people talk quite loudly too. We Indians are a very expressive lot and we are not ashamed to laugh or talk loudly if we have to. Especially if you come from a country with disciplined crowds speaking at low volume, the sheer variety of Indian noises can take some time getting used to. If you wish to avoid crowds as much as possible, it is a good idea to choose hotels that are a little away from tourist areas or near populous places like bazaars. While the hotel may be well-run and quiet, you may often be badgered by noises from outside, unless you are in an AC room with sealed windows.

Many Indians grow up without a sense of personal space, due to crowded home surroundings or extended families, so brace yourselves if people get too close at railway stations or buses. Most of the time, it's nothing. Is just the way people are in India? People like to live communally.

But if people are too pushy then be firm though when dealing with crowds at service lines or you may not get the service you are looking for. Stick to your place politely but avoid getting pushed around or getting into altercations. Say 'No' firmly ('Nahin' in Hindi) to unwanted attention. Also, women need to be careful and firm about personal space sometimes, as some men may resort to groping in overcrowded buses.

These guidelines apart, one of the best ways to deal with Indian crowds is to generally give in and enjoy the flow. For people who enjoy clicking amazing photo opportunities abound at crowded traditional Indian bazaars, pilgrimage spots, and so on will love it. So, take your time and you will gradually acclimatize to the Indian crowd, its colors, cacophony and general liveliness.

Crowd can be a good thing

Finally it is a good idea to stay with the crowds. Sometimes it's safer to be where there are a lot of people around. When you get in danger or you feel you are being harassed by someone then you can raise you voice and call for help. You will realize that people are more than willing to help. So crowds may not always be a bad thing.

28. How to keep your money and passport safe?

Wherever you travel, you have to keep money and your passport safe otherwise you are going to get in deep mess. Needless to say, in India, a land of a billion plus with so many people brushing by you on roads, at railway stations and so on, this becomes even more important. But there is no need to get paranoid about keep your money and passport safe. Just because you cannot avoid crowds in India, that doesn't mean you stay cooped up in this gloriously chaotic land. Avoid carrying your money and valuables into very crowded places as much as you can and just take some basic precautions.

Here is a quick traveler's guide to keeping your money and passport safe in India.

Small money in a small place

A precaution many people use is to keep small money in small places. Many people prefer to carry a small purse for the small change. For example, if you are going about the town, say to go a restaurant or visiting an Indian friend, you surely do not need to carry all your money or valuables with you all the time. Use small handy pouches instead for your everyday use and some paper money for the road, so that even if you are robbed, it's not a big loss. In addition, keep your money distributed in different purses and bags as an added safety measure.

Safety precautions for bags

If you keep your money and passport in a big bag, make sure it's within a deep pocket. You can also have a secret flap in your trolley bag in which to tuck your money and passport safely. Have locks for the zippers on the outside of the bags. Keep the tiny keys in a safe place where you can easily find them.

Passport safety

Ideally, keep your passport and important identification documents on your person. Also have a place where you can store passport information and a few passport size photos safely. Have copies of important documents in file or store on online facilities for safe-keeping. Another thing you can do is to email yourself a scanned copy of the passport so that you can print one out when required.

Safety in hotels

Whether you stay in a roadside inn or a 5-star hotel the safety precautions you take and basic commonsense are going to the same everywhere. If the bags containing your main money are in your hotel room, have padlocks or cable locks for the door. This way, you have peace of mind even when you are out travelling in the city. Many medium-range or luxury hotels let you pay extra for safe deposit boxes. You can also purchase a portable travel safe and store your important items, padlocked, during the trip.

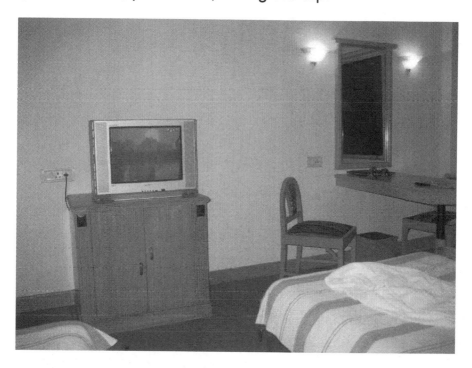

Have backups

Use your debit card if you can for travelling, instead of carrying large sums of money that can be easily robbed. Get two copies of your debit cards with one card for your travelling purpose and the other safe back at home. If the bag with one debit card is stolen then you know you have a backup in place. An interesting idea to dissuade pickpockets can be to carry two wallets. One would be a dummy while the other one carries your travel money. You can keep these in separate pockets while you travel. Many travelers swear by traveler's cheque. They are advised to keep a record of the cheque numbers.

Avoid leather for your purse

Sometimes in Hindu temples you are not allowed to wear anything made of leather into the premises, which can include your shoes, belt, and purse/wallet. If do have any leather items on you then you might have to deposit it while you are taking a tour of the temple. To avoid having to let go of your leather purse during the tour of the temple, just use purses made of other materials.

Keep your luggage close

Always keep an eye on your luggage especially during transit. Buses often have spaces to store luggage on top. Avoid putting bags with valuables there. Also, it's better to travel light, avoid the service of porters and manage your own luggage.

Then there are traditional techniques like socks with a secret compartment, money belts to notes stashed safely, carrying the big notes in a cloth pouch against the skin, etc, to keep money, passport, credit card etc. safe. If are doing a lot of travelling then you will come up with your own improvisations on some of the commonly used tactics for safe-keeping of valuables on trips.

29. Safety tips for women

Sadly in recent years a huge number of horror stories have come up regarding how unsafe India is for women. The truth is that travelling in India is no more and no less safe than travelling elsewhere although there are variable pockets of risk in some places. Whether you are travelling in a women's group or as a single woman, there are numerous ways in which you can protect yourself while on your tour to India.

Here are some safety tips

At hotels

Try to select hotels that are well-known and have a good review. If you look online, there are many sites where people rate hotels and leave reviews. One way to find out about a hotel is to Google the hotel. Anything that has been written online about the hotel should appear and you can judge it for yourself.

A few top-of-the-line hotels even have separate wings with rooms dedicated to women. As far as you can, avoid hotels in shabby locations. They may be cheap but safety wise, end up costing you more in the long run. This applies whether you're travelling in India or elsewhere in the world.

On trains

Trains are convenient and economical for travelling over long distances. In many cases, local or suburban trains connect big cities to places in the suburbs. Trains often have compartments which are meant for women passengers and you can choose these over and above general compartments. But how do you know which are compartments for women? Usually the women's-only compartment in trains is third from last or you can just stand where many women are waiting on the platform. You will find a lot of women clustered in one part of the platform, just go and ask if they are waiting for the women's only compartment. If you have a long wait at the station, say for several hours to catch a connecting train, you can go the Rail Yatri Nivas or waiting room available at most stations.

On other forms of public transport

Buses are commonly used for travelling within the city and for inter-city travel. If you are taking a bus, especially in state-run buses, several seats are meant for women passengers. If you plan to take overnight buses or those connecting cities, pre-book if you have the option. Taxis give you the luxury of travelling privately between places, but it's a good idea to know the route before hand to avoid being duped or overcharged by the driver. Prepaid taxis or taxi rental services are usually a safer option than hiring taxis off the street.

In tourist spots

In most tourist spots of India there is some sort of government surveillance but it is also a good idea to look out for your own safety. Usually special police forces patrol tourist areas, looking for signs of trouble or misbehavior and you can report to them if you feel unsafe. Also, try to follow regular safety precautions like not being in unlit areas after dark. Do not just go off with a stranger and if you are going out partying, stick to drinking with people you can trust.

Using the mobile phone for safety

These days, technology can also help keep you safe as a woman tourist. In general, wherever you travel, have a safe point of contact you can call in an emergency, and let friends if you have any in the country know of your whereabouts. You can always let your hotel know about your whereabouts. Tell people at the reception that you might call them if you get in trouble or if you need anything. In most cases, they will be willing to help.

Here's a tip - Set up a Speed Dial system on your mobile phone for emergency numbers like 100 for the Police or 108 for general emergencies in southern cities like Bengaluru, Hyderabad, Chennai and Kochi. Also, note the toll-free number nationwide to report sexual harassment or other issues you face as a traveller.

In taxis if you feel unsafe, an oft-used tip is to pretend to call a friend and keep talking. Also, note the number of the taxi you are travelling in and pretend to say it aloud to your friend at the other end of the line. Get off at the nearest police station or the nearest crowded public area you can find. While Indian crowds can be intimidating, in emergency situations, they act as a safety net preventing miscreants from following you. Also if you can have a pepper spray bottle or something similar handy keep one as it can work to ward off possible attacks. In case of any trouble, head to your country consulate without wasting time or at least phone them up. You can get their phone number from the internet.

A few practical strategies like these can help you enjoy a safe tour in India. It is always better to be safe than sorry.

30. Travelling with kids in India

Are you planning to tour India with children? Contrary to what you may have been told, it is fun and exciting to travel with kids in India. With so many colors and interesting flavors and sights, your kids are sure to have lots of fun. All it needs is a bit of homework, like you would normally do if you were going on a tour in any part of the world. Indians are often a family oriented lot so you will find them warm and friendly with your kids.

Here is a look at some factors to keep in mind if you are planning a kids-friendly vacation in India.

Research the amenities

Depending on how old the child is, you may need to look into the amenities aspect at every stage. Very small children who stay in their cots need extra care. In India, kids below 2 years get to travel at 10% of the adult airfare and below 12 years of age it's half the price of a grown-up's ticket. So, you can save considerably on airfares if you plan to do different cities on one Indian trip. Indian restaurants usually do not have high chairs, so you can pack a portable high chair to enjoy fuss-free mealtimes if you are eating out in India. In hotels, kids below 12 years of age stay free of cost with adults in a room.

Updated medical protection

India is often hot, dusty and very crowded so it's quite easy for kids to fall ill. Make sure your kids have all their immunizations updated and take the advice of your doctor before coming to India. If special immunizations are recommended by the doctor for rabies, get those completed before flying out to India.

A common ailment many small kids suffer in their first few days in the country is diarrhea. Boil and sterilize all the water and use it to disinfect bowls and spoons if you have an infant with you. Most decent hotels will have kettles but you can consider bringing your own travel or mini kettle.

If you travel with kids, always pack a portable medical kit with basics like band-aids, thermometers and fever medications from your own country. In addition, carry some medicines for diarrhea. It is also a good idea to prepare a rehydration therapy. Diarrhea and other stomach infections cause a lot of water to drain out of the system and oral hydration solutions like ORS (Oral Rehydration Solution) made of salt, sugar and water, fed at regular intervals to the child can compensate for this loss. In case emergency medical treatment is needed, your hotel can usually recommend a nearby hospital or call a doctor for you. Alternatively, wherever you are travelling, list some local hospital names and phone numbers for safe-keeping when you reach your destination. Make sure you buy travel insurance and keep their emergency numbers at hand so that if you do need it, you can call them quickly.

In-transit comfort

For those not used to very big crowds, the cluttered roads in Indian cities and towns can be quite a shock. People going in every direction, the frequent absence of pedestrian-friendly spaces and a free-for-all attitude on the streets can be discomfiting for a small child. Pack light and avoid strollers as you usually don't have space for them on crowded roads. Instead, opt for back-packs which have child-carrier provisions. These backpacks also work great if you are going on light treks or planning hikes.

Food discomfort

One of the strangest elements of a foreign culture for small kids is the food. If the child is very small, you should bring your own baby food that you can either carry with you as you travel. With older kids, the spicy Indian food may be too difficult to digest. Hotels often entertain special requests for the basics like boiled rice and veggies and pulses which are all great nutritious items that are of low-spice and easy on small tummies.

Handling crowds

Your kids may often be the focus of excitement and attention on Indian roads and you may find inquisitive and friendly locals, eager to chat to your child. There may even be requests to click photos of your children. If you are uncomfortable with this attention, it is okay to indicate this with a shake of the head and walk on. It is also a good idea to explain to kids that strangers may approach them in India, and it's nothing to worry about but they should not take anything from them. This is not unusual as Indians often enjoy interacting with small kids. But your child must understand not to take anything from a stranger and definitely not eat anything a stranger gives.

Keep an eye on them

As previously mentioned, India is a big country with a lot of people. The roads can be crowded so you must keep an eye on your children all the time. Hold their hands when on the streets and do not let them wander off. Sadly abductions of children do happen hence you must make sure that your children are never out of your site at any time.

Give them a camera

Why not give them a camera. You can buy a cheap digital camera and you never know what pictures they might take. This way, they will not get bored and bother you to go back to the hotel.

Give them the hotel details

If your child is old enough to remember things than make sure they know which hotel and area they are staying in. Alternatively, you can write your name, address, contact details and the name of the hotel and put it in their pocket. If they did get lost, at least the police will be able to call you or the hotel.

31. Types of places to shop

India is a shopping haven for many. Although prices of goods have increased in recent years, it is still relatively cheaper to shop in India. There are numerous places where you can shop.

Let's take a look at some of them

Shopping malls

A relatively new shopping format in India, malls have caught on in a big way as a weekend hangout for families and young people. A typical shopping mall is air-conditioned, multi-level, has security measures, accepts cash and credit/debit cards, and depending on the size of the mall, it may even have a movie hall or multiplex, a few take-away joints or sit-down restaurants along with a cluster of shops selling local or international brands. Basically it's a like a town centre you get in Great Britain.

Stand-alone departmental stores offering various brands of products are found in big cities. The air-conditioned arrangements and computerized handling of cash or credit/debit cards allow shopping in a hassle-free manner. They often do home deliveries which is convenient for many working couples or busy families.

Items you may get at well-equipped Indian shopping malls include things like frozen food items, clothing, accessories, electronic goods etc. You will certainly feel at home in these shopping malls.

Street shops

These shops are everywhere. These mom and pop stores are called "kirana" stores in many places in India. Grocery stores owned by individuals sell limited stocks of local merchandise and daily use items. You find all sorts of thing even items you may not find in the shopping malls. If you wanted to buy basic items like soap, toothpaste etc you can buy them in these types of stores.

In many old Indian cities, you may find stalls lining narrow gullies where you get spices, bangles, metal idols, decorative items etc. These are the stalls you want to try!

The government has its own emporium outlets by the street in many tourist-friendly cities. In these emporiums you can pick up handicrafts, textiles and other traditional items at standard rates. Most of the time, the prices are fixed by the government although you may get a discount on some items – just feel free to ask at the counter.

Sweet and snack shops

Great thing about India is its variety of sweets and snacks. Some of the popular ones include ras malai, gulab jamun, chole bhature, chena pais, jalebi, samosa, chaat and so on.

[147]

You find many shops specializing in traditional Indian sweets, drinks, snacks and fried dishes. These are many stand alone shops where you can try sweets and snacks on the go. They are much safer as far as hygiene is concerned. If the shop is full of people then this means that they are a popular outlet and they have a huge turnover of ingredients. Feel free to ask about the various types of sweets and snacks. In many of these sweet shops, you will find that the handlers will be using gloves and therefore there is harm in trying the sweets and snacks on offer. In fact, I suggest you try them. Many of them will also have burgers and cakes in western styled – just ask who ever is serving.

Pavement stalls

People set up their wares either in carts, makeshift stalls or on the pavement, and carry the unsold products and their 'stall' home at the end of the day. You can pick up different items like clothes, accessories, toys, plastic items like combs, buckets, mugs etc. at these stalls.

Bazaars

If you want to get fresh local produce such as fruits, vegetables, fish and meat then Indian bazaars give you that option in some cities and towns. The supplies come from the rural locations that are close to the big cities. The bazaar, often called a "subzi mandi" in Northern India, if it sells only fruits and veggies, usually consists of sprawling makeshift arrangements on the footpath. The sellers may also have their own basic stalls to display the items tastefully. The colors, chaos, smells usually full with bargainers and sellers make these Indian bazaars a quite an experience.

Besides bazaars for fresh food items, many cities have traditional specialized bazaars such as Chor Bazaar for antique goods in Delhi or the Janpath in Delhi has the best of street shopping you can experience.

Markets

Many cities have markets in which stalls are assigned to the owners. A few famous markets are New Market in Kolkata (in a building), the open-air Sarojini Nagar Market in New Delhi etc. where you get great bargains on various items. You may have to sweat quite a bit as many markets are not air-conditioned.

Flea markets

At flea markets, often organized in Goa and some other places in India, you can buy second-hand or first-hand items, at dirt-cheap rates. Many flea markets are weekly or set up in the evening or morning. You will have to enquire with your hotel or tour organizer about local flea markets.

Haats

Haats are a traditional place to buy and sell and are set up at specific times, such as once a week under a tree or on the side of the road, depending on the local arrangements. Usually, people come from nearby villages to buy the certain merchandises on offer at these haats which may include local handicrafts, toys, household utilitarian devices, cattle etc. depending on the kind of haat. One of the most famous haat is the Dilli Haat of Delhi showcasing the best of Indian craftsmanship in one open-air plaza. I highly recommend going there if you are considering buying local Indian products that can range from silk and wool fabrics to camel hide footwear. It's quite a treat.

Fairs

Fairs are places where you shop plus enjoy a festive carnival like atmosphere. Many of these fairs have giant wheels and merry-go-rounds for children. An Indian fair, called a 'mela' usually refers to a gathering of people who meet for a common purpose, usually to buy and sell, entertain or take part in a religious ceremony. Many melas are ages-old and go back centuries. Many of them were started by the local aristocrat or even the people of the place to celebrate a religious or social occasion. Depending on the customs, these fairs continue for a week or a month, and are often seasonal or annual. In melas, people are in a festive mood and you will get to try local snacks, sweet dishes, traditional handicrafts etc. Fairs in India can range from books fairs such as the Patna Book Fair to religious one such as the famous Pushkar Fair of Rajasthan. The most famous mela of them all is the Kumbh Mela which is considered as the largest gathering of human beings on the planet. It is in this mela that Hindus bathe in the River Ganges to wash their sins away.

32. How to bargain?

India is a country where people bargain for almost everything and everywhere and when it comes to shopping at the bazaars then it becomes even more blatant. In recent years, India has seen the opening of large departmental stores in urban centers of the country which are sadly not conducive to bargaining. But the small stores and road-side stalls are a great testing ground! If you want to plunge into the mad spree of bargain shopping in India, check out these free-style bargaining suggestions.

Bargaining is an art

A suggestion is to spend time soaking in the atmosphere in the crowded bazaars and observing what the locals are doing. Not every local is great at bargaining, so you need to observe the gestures, the body language and the psychological tactics that are being used by all sides. Being a tourist, you will stand out and sellers will most certainly increase the price. Therefore you will also need to apply your own unique strategy because bargaining as a foreigner will certainly be a lot harder and more challenging.

Remember the price differences

Indians, especially the ones who shop in street markets are usually quite price sensitive so the prices are decided by vendors keeping the customers in mind. Remember though that the prices for foreigners are usually much higher, whether in Colaba at the Causeway or in Gariahat in Kolkata or Javeri Bazaaar in Delhi. If the local salesperson can figure out you are a foreigner from your accent, speech intonation, appearance etc., they will automatically charge you higher for the same object. But you can't really camouflage your natural looks? That'd be absurd. You can however let the vendor know that you won't be standing for any price discrimination or better still, go to the market with a local friend if you have any.

Know the game

Bargaining is about negotiating the price that's stated upfront by the vendor. The truth is that both the vendor and the customer know that they are playing a kind of game. One of the first things hardcore bargainers do is to quote a price that's just half the stated price. Then the vendor quotes another price, and this way the game continues till the price satisfies both parties, and usually both feel they have won. The feel-good factor is often at the root of most bargaining.

Develop a toughened exterior

Sometimes a toughened exterior is what makes bargaining successfully. Some common gestures that seasoned bargainers use is to shrug, pretend indifference, and never show that they are eager to buy an item. Also, be sure that your body language remains neutral. Seasoned vendors are quite skilled in interpreting their customers' body language.

The tactic I have seen with my grandmother, a hardcore bargainer if there was ever any, is to actually walk away once she has stated the 'final price'. This usually refers to the last price that the would-be-customer agrees to pay. Usually, as soon as my grandmother starts walking away, the vendor calls her back, telling her that despite the risk of running a grave loss, the quoted price is fine. You need to be really confident to pull this one off.

On the other hand, if you really like the item, have walked on and the vendor does not call you back, you know you have quoted a price that's too low. Then you have two options: Keep walking on and don't buy the item. Or, risk losing face and return.

Know the value of what you are bargaining for

Often it is okay to pay a little extra for handmade goods, or those which you can see that has required a lot of skill and patience. A suggestion: Roam the locality and browse the places selling similar products so you get an idea of the average price. Bargaining well often needs a great deal of patience and insight into local market conditions. Avoid jumping excitedly at the items at the first store you come across. Spend your time studying the market carefully, and then step gradually into the game fine-tuning your bargaining tactics as you go along with the situation.

Most people who are seasoned at bargaining will have a host of pet tactics that they use. You can find out some of these tactics by talking to locals. Also, it is definitely a good idea to know some of the local language – otherwise it's difficult to find common ground with the vendor – and you just have to settle for shopping without bargaining.

I have included some more shopping Hindi words, phrases and sentences.

Price – Daam

Kitna – How much

How much is this –Ye kitnay ka hai

Lower the price – Daam kum keejiye

Price is too mich – Daam bahut hai

I don't want this –Mujhe nahi chaheeye

I want this one – Mujhe ye wala chaeeye

Nahi –No

Yes - Haa

Shop – Dukaan

Clothes shop – Kapray ka dukaan

Do you have medium size – Kya aap ke pass medium size hai

Small - Chota

Big – Baara

I have included some haggling words and phrases on my website with audio here http://www.shalusharma.com/how-to-bargain-in-india/.

33. What should women wear?

Every country has a certain cultural code and India is a country with many of these. In some parts of the country particularly the remote areas and smaller towns, women often wear clothing that covers their skin. In big cities, you often find a vibrant nightlife and opportunities for partying in addition to the freedom to wear revealing clothes if you like. No matter which part of India you are, it is a good idea to observe the locals and try to adapt a bit and blend in instead of sticking out in terms of clothing.

Wherever you travel in India, you're bound to come across all kinds of clothing. While Western clothes like jeans are popular amongst the young women of the cities and towns, traditional clothes are a common sight too. In the North-East you find stitched traditional clothes in many colorful and existing patterns. The desert women in the Western part of the country such as the remote areas of Rajasthan have colorful clothing such as 'ghagra' kind of full long skirt teamed with short blouse known as 'choli'.

Given this immense variety of clothes, what sort of clothes would be good to wear to India? In fact, you can wear different kinds of clothes depending on the location and situation.

Here are some suggestions and you can improvise as you go along.

The salwar kameez, a set comprising of loose pants or pyajamas and an upper tunic with a narrow often thin scarf called a dupatta is very popular in most parts of India. If you are going to be doing some serious amount of travelling, you can incorporate leggings and an upper tunic as a part of your wardrobe. Team this with a short colorful scarf and add some bling to your arms or neck if you like. This can be your makeshift salwar kameez, keeping your skin cool and comfortably protected from the heat while letting you roam more or less dressed in local style in rural areas especially in the north of the country.

If leggings do not work for you, you can try wearing pajamas that are gathered at the ankle locally known as harem trousers. These are flowy and allow enough air to pass through to your skin, while adding a bit of color to your wardrobe. Harem trousers go well with medium length tees.

Trousers made of denim or patterned cloth combined with T-shirts is another comfortable option while travelling to India. Keep some colorful scarves handy. You can use the scarves to cover your arms or protect your hair from the dust when you are travelling in public transport like a speeding auto-rickshaw. Since many parts of India dress conservatively, it is a good idea to wear tees that are not too close-fitting or those that reveal too much skin. It is a good idea for trousers not to be too skin tight either. You can make an exception for places like Goa that gets a lot of foreign visitors and the locals are used to seeing foreign tourists in larger numbers. Cut-offs is fine usually those that end at mid-calf length but not too abbreviated.

Skirts are a good option for travelling in India as they keep your legs cool and comfortable. Unless you are at parties or places where there are many foreigners, wear the skirt in a conservative fashion. This means - no wide slide slits, or too short skirts ending at thigh length. If you do wear very short skirts, incorporate leggings or stockings. An alternative that is cooler in the hot, sticky climate of India is a sarong. These brightly patterned wrap-around skirts, ending at mid-calf length or at the ankle were originally worn by Burmese women. They look graceful when worn with a sleeveless top and a short scarf or with a long loose tunic with three-quarter sleeves.

As for footwear, try to avoid heels or shoes with very narrow points except at parties. Indian roads can often be precarious and you may get a nasty fall. Instead, settle for comfortable open-toe sandals, sneakers, or floaters, depending on the dress you are wearing.

The clothes may be various but one factor uniting them all is color. Indians love bright colors, patterns, embellishments and embroidery styles are often part of what they wear. So, add silver or bead accessories to pep up your clothes, go for caps or wrap scarves bandana style around your head. Don't be afraid to dress in bright and colorful clothes and feel the vibrant spirit of India as you enjoy the wanderlust.

Try to avoid gold ornaments. If you do wear gold chains make sure you have them tucked inside the clothing and away from sight. There have been incidences of chain-snacking, so do be careful.

34. What should men wear?

India has plenty of places to explore but they all involve touring around often in hot, humid and dusty conditions. As a man, if you are very used to heavy nylon, woolen or polyester clothing, forget about them and incorporate more lightweight fabrics for your Indian tour. If you are going to the higher colder regions of India, you do need warm clothes but apart from these locations, you can get by fine with cool, light fabrics that help your skin to breathe.

What kind of clothes is comfortable and suitable for Indian tours? Here's what you can do.

Cotton and linen are good choices for most part of India in terms of fabric. These have traditionally been a part of Indian wardrobes and you will feel much cooler and comfortable wearing them compared to heavy cotswool or polyester-based fabrics.

While touring India, discard trousers made of heavy fabrics.
These are more suited for cooler climates and get sticky after
a few hours in the humid sub-tropical Indian climate. You can
wear these for formal occasions or in places you know will be
air-conditioned. For regular wear, try lightweight cotton
trousers in neutral shades, checks or patterns that you like.
You can wear them for longer periods and they keep your
legs protected from the heat. You can also wear shorts that
cover at least three quarters of your legs. Leave the
extremely short 'burmudas' or shorts only for the beaches.
These are usually not worn in cities or towns and you will be
sticking out among the more conservatively dressed Indians.
Jeans are usually fine and they work well in India. But if you
are wearing denim trousers, they should not be too low-slung
that let's your briefs peep out. Dress in long or medium
length jeans. You can also wear combo pants with multiple
pockets to keep your valuables hidden and safe from pick
pockets.

In terms of footwear, it is a good idea to think in terms of open, free and cool. If you keep your feet covered in heavy shoes especially those made of leather; your feet will usually end up sticky and smelly, even before the day is over. You can pick up rubber sandals known as 'chappals' in most parts of India. These are colorful and waterproof, and sturdy. You can also go for floaters to let your feet breathe or try sneakers with socks to keep your feet protected from the dust and grime. Given the humid climate in many parts of India, cotton socks is a better option compared to nylon ones. Let your feet get enough air from time to time by keeping them shoe-less. You can also buy traditional Indian shoes called jooti's that are flat styled sandals with narrow pointed toes curling slightly upward. You find jootis at many traditional Indian footwear stores especially in the northern part of the country or in government-run emporiums in bigger cities. With jootis or other traditional footwear, you do not need to wear socks.

Wear half-sleeved shirts or T-shirt, as full-sleeved clothes may be too hot and uncomfortable. A better idea is to fold your sleeves during the day and wear them during the night to protect yourself from mosquitoes.

If you are coming to the country in summer or touring very hot regions, you can also wear sleeveless T-shirts. Round-neck or V-neck T-shirts are fine. It is a good idea not to wear very deep-cut V-necks though. Alternatively, you can go for full-sleeved but very loose tees to cover your arms from the heat. You just have to see what works best for you.

The "kurta" is a Middle-Eastern garment which is slightly long kind of shirt that ends near or a little above the knee and comes with loose long sleeves. These are worn with pajamas. You can also get experimental and wear a kurta with long denim trousers. You can find a variety of colorful kurtas in long and medium-length variety selling in shops and on the roadside in most parts of India. Indian men are not afraid of colors in their traditional wear therefore you too can pick up colorfully checked or patterned kurtas. In fact, these kurtas will make you blend in the Indian crowd quite easily.

Incorporate short scarves in your Indian wardrobe. You can wear these casually wrapped around your neck, draped over your chest or simply tie your head with the cloth to protect yourself from the dust. Scarves also add color and help to layer your clothes while touring India.

Travel light with a few basic essentials of clothing, like denim trousers and T-shirts. Pick up some colorful clothing in India and do not be afraid to wear Indian clothes. Just buy a few and try them on and blend in.

35. Say no to bhang and other drugs

Lots of travelers are coming to India to try the "bhang". Let me give you an idea what exactly bhang is and if it is safe or not to try.

Bhang is a cheap intoxicant derived from the leaves of the cannabis plant which is generally smoked and also consumed as a drink in India. Bhang has been consumed in India for ages. Bhang is traditionally consumed on festivals like Mahashivratri and Holi. In fact on festivals like Holi, it has become a tradition to drink Lassi (yogurt based drink) with bhang mixed in it. Bhang is also used as a sleeping aid and an appetizer and is a part of many ayurvedic medicines. Though like most drugs it has been often misused. Bhang golis (balls) are easily available in paan-shops as "bhola" or "munakka", it is often used as a fun booster but overdose of bhang can be life threatening.

Bhang is not something which is new in society; it has been used for centuries and is culturally ingrained in the culture of India. There is a mythological connection to bhang as well. It is said that Lord Shiva consumed bhang on his wedding day and hence his disciples (worshippers) consume it as well. On the occasion of Holi, it is mixed with sweets such as laddoos, lassi, jalebi, pakoras and thandai to liven the spirits of the people. Few states even have government authorized bhang shops while some have banned it completely but despite the bans it is as easily available.

Bhang is one of the most easily available drugs in India, though not as dangerous as other drugs but can have dire consequences if one gets addicted. There have been a rise in cases of drug abuse where youngsters start with this drug and then proceed to more harder types of drugs hence it is not encouraged. Kids in school and colleges get attracted on the drug due to its availability and get themselves knowingly/unknowingly involved in a mess. These kids start with bhang and ultimately get addicted and then with time move on other dangerous drugs like cocaine, hash or heroine. Also in some late night parties drugs are common and so attract lot of inquisitive youths who are ready to experiment with different things.

Drugs were not common in parties of late but with rise of modern culture, it has become a potential threat among the proactive youth in the country. Rave parties are becoming famous and are attract a lot of celebrities. Also the drug mafia has been spreading its wings rapidly especially in the metropolitan cities. The source of drugs in India is mainly domestic and rest is imported mainly from Afghanistan and is smuggled through the porous Nepal border.

The menace of drugs and its trafficking has grown viciously in last few years. The beautiful coastal state of Goa has become the drug paradise in India with almost every drug type is readily available without any hitch. The drug market in Goa is controlled by Israelis as claimed by the Goa Government and now dominant Russians and Nigerians (recent news) run the show with the support of locals (there has been a crackdown recently by the Goa Government in recent years).

Everyone has their own defined market with no interference in other's business. A report claims that an average youth from Goa starts abusing drugs at the age of 14 with more readily drugs like ganja or marijuana but later moves on to fatal drugs like heroin, cocaine or LSD. This menace of drug trafficking started in 1970s and has grown ever since.

Not only Goa, drug abuse has escalated vigorously in all tourist spots especially the mountains of North India. Himachal Pradesh has become the capital for drug production. In this state, cannabis is grown in acres of land without any apprehensions. A town named Kasol in Kullu dominates the drug production. The town has around 3000 foreign nationals who run the drug racket. The situation is so grave that other nearby villages has started competing in the trade. This drug haven is run allegedly by Israelis drug gangs and smuggled to metropolitan cities and Goa and even exported. The situation in Kashmir is similar too where drugs continue to ruin thousands of lives.

The most disturbing fact is that the government in many states despite knowing the full details of the situation is still turning a blind eye towards this heinous crime. There are many officials who are not directly involved in this mess but aid the peddlers and patronize them. The Anti-narcotics department despite knowing everything is not really taking any concrete steps to curb the situation. Some say that that they have insiders who might also be involved in drug peddling. If the administration doesn't take any action, this menace of drug abuse will remain.

If you really wanted to consume some bhang, the best place is from the government approved bhang shops of Varanasi at your own risk. But my recommendation is that you stay away from all drugs completely without any reservation. The last thing you want is to take drugs or get involved in any sort of drug abuse or trafficking. Just say no and stay away.

References

Goa: Cop-neta nexus in tango with drugs mafia, says House report – firstpost.com

Sex, drugs and narcotics: How peaceful Himachal Pradesh became a rave haven awash with foreign mafia - dailymail.co.uk

Turf wars tarnish Goa's paradise image - theguardian.com

36. Common Hindi words and phrases

Although English is fine in most parts of India, there are some sections of Indian society that do not know any English at all. They usually will be bell-boys of hotel rooms, rickshaw drivers, porters and so on. So it it's a good idea to polish on some basic Hindi words and phrases for your travels India. Hindi is not spoken everywhere in India, although most places in India, there are people who are able to speak in Hindi. So if you do manage to speak some of these Hindi words and phrases, you will still be understood in most parts of India expect the very Southern states of India namely Karnataka, Kerala and Tamil Nadu.

Here are some common Hindi words, phrases and sentences.

Hello – Namaste

Thank you – Sukriya or Dhanyevaad

Who are you - Aap kaun hai

Sorry – Maaf Keejiye

Please – Kripya

What is your name - Aap ka kya naam hai

Where are you from - Aap kaha se hai

Where are you going - Aap kaha ja rahe hai

This is my seat - Ye mera seat hai

This is mine - Ye mera hai

This is yours - Ye aap ka hai

This suitcase is mine – Ye suitcase mera hai

Where is my luggage – Mera saamaan kaha hai

Morning – Subah

Night – Raat

Today- Aaj

Tomorrow – Kaal

Temple – Mandir

Mosque – Masjid

Okay – Thik hai

Let's go - Chalo

Stop – Ruko

Clothes – Kapra

These clothes are mine - Ye mera kapra hai

Towel – Tauliya

Toilet - Suchalay

Soap – Sabun

I want to go to the toilet – Mujhe sauchalay jana hai

Food - Khana

Chapattis - Roti

Rice - Chawal

Lentils - Daal

Sugar – Cheeni

Water - Paani

Tea – Chai

Vegetables – Subjee

Fruits -Phal

I want a plate of rice – Mujhe ek plate rice chaiye

I want a plate of chicken curry – Mujhe ek plate chicken curry chahiye

I want a plate of vegetable curry –Muhe subji ke curry chahiye

I want 1 chapatti – Mujhe ek roti chahiye

Where is the railway station - Railway station kaha hai

Where is the hotel - Hotel kaha hai

Where is the taxi stand – Taxi stand kaha hai

Where is the driver – Driver kaha hai

Where can I buy tickets – Tickets kaha milega

What is the price of a ticket – Ek ticket ka daam kya hai

Give me one ticket - Ek ticket chahiye

Give me two tickets - Do ticket chahiye

How much is this - Ye kitnay ka hai

I want this - Mujhe ye chahiye

Lower the price - Daam kum keejiye

One - Ek

Two - Do

Three - Teen

Four - Char

Five - Panch

Six - Chhai

Seven - Saath

Eight - Aath

Nine - Nau

Ten - Dus

37. Message from the author

Thank you for buying my book. I hope after reading this book, you would now be more comfortable for your travels in India.

Remember India is not as frightening as it seems. As long you take the precautions mentioned in the book, you're going to be fine. Be careful with your food. Food in India can be very spicy and can take you by surprise. You just have to ask the waiters to make it less spicy if you aren't comfortable with Indian food. Women's safety is of major concern. Women should not wear too revealing clothes and should not ideally venture out alone after dark. But all in all, India is a relatively safe and good tourist destination and if adequate precautions are taken, I do not see any reason for concern.

If you have any questions on India or travelling to India, then feel free to ask me a question on my website http://www.shalusharma.com and feel free to subscribe to my newsletter for travel related news on India http://www.shalusharma.com/subscribe. I will try my best to answer any questions that you might have.

Here are my other books that you might consider buying:

India Travel Survival Guide For Women - ISBN-10: 149122648X
Essential Hindi Words And Phrases For Travelers To India - ISBN-10: 1492752517
Hinduism For Kids: Beliefs And Practices - ISBN-10: 1495370429
India For Kids: Amazing Facts About India - ISBN-10: 149470997X

Best wishes to you and have a nice and safe trip to India. Feel free to shoot me an email if you want any help.

Take care...

Shalu Sharma

Essential India Travel Guide: Travel Tips And Practical Information

By

Shalu Sharma

Table of Contents